150 50 PROJECT

TRANSFORMING AMERICAN'S EDUCATION SYSTEM

CYNTHIA PRICE

authorHOUSE®

AuthorHouse™
1663 Liberty Drive
Bloomington, IN 47403
www.authorhouse.com
Phone: 833-262-8899

Published by AuthorHouse 02/23/2024

ISBN: 979-8-8230-2088-6 (sc)
ISBN: 979-8-8230-2087-9 (hc)
ISBN: 979-8-8230-2089-3 (e)

Library of Congress Control Number: 2024901412

Print information available on the last page.

This book is printed on acid-free paper.

CONTENTS

Part II
Research of Diversity Equity and Inclusion

CHAPTER 1
THE 150-50 PROJECT

The three theoretical frameworks of Urie Bronfenbrenner (ecological theory), Pierre Bourdieu (cultural capital), and James Coleman (social capital) encourage teachers to build relationships with students. Relationships with students are built through awareness of how to achieve and maintain academic success, positive school relationships, and community awareness. Another area of significance is the development of students' skills to lead the school in meetings, panel discussions, seminars, speech contests, and positive school rallies that will reflect students' input. Positive student relationships provide alternative solutions to problems that students encounter at school and in the community.

There is a need to create a pathway for youth to voice their opinions about the disparities that they face today. The teacher-student relationship can foster solutions/alternatives for conflict resolutions in school and community and begin a positive dialogue for youth to connect with role models in the school and community. Students learn how to interact with the school and community in a positive environment; at the same time, they achieve success/rewards for their outstanding accomplishments in academics, athletics, event planning, group participation, group coordination, and conflict resolution.

Bronfenbrenner discusses the child through the framework of individual systems (microsystem, mesosystem, exosystem, and macrosystem).

My research points to the mesosystem, exosystem, and macrosystem. These systems are linked, and student processes take place between the developing person and the relationships between home, school, community, and workplace. Studies of children and adults in life settings, life implications, are now commonplace in the research literature on human development. This model holds assumptions about the ways in which parental involvement, school factors, and socioeconomic status interact to influence academic achievement. Leonard's (2012) reading also reveals the network relationships of the mesosystem. According to Leonard, teenagers may focus on school, home, and peer relationship networks. One or more of these common threads exist in building relationships with students.

Pierre Bourdieu (cultural capital) and James Coleman (social capital) are connected to Bronfenbrenner (ecological theory). Bourdieu's cultural capital connects to Bronfenbrenner at three levels. The *embodied* state of cultural capital is defined as the long-lasting dispositions of the mind and body (microsystem and mesosystem). The *objectified* state of cultural capital exists in forms of cultural goods, pictures, books, and instruments (mesosystem). The *institutionalized* state of cultural capital exists in academic qualifications or means of measurement of cultural goods (Bourdieu 1973, 51), which is connected to the exosystem and macrosystem. James Coleman's theory of social capital exists in forms of name, tribe, school, and geographical, economic, and social space, which applies to Bronfenbrenner's entire theory. Opportunities for increased capital depend on networks available and used by the individual. These theories are the foundation of the 150-50 Project.

The 150-50 Project encompasses building positive relationships among teachers, students, and community. Teachers conduct action research that nurtures the importance of community partners and presents ideas of how to close the achievement gap among minority students. The framework of the project works to increase literacy by creating diversity through cultural learning, creating diversity through building relationships with students, and creating diversity through a community of educators that recognizes culture identities of students.

One teacher has the potential to reach 150 students a day. The teacher teaches five times a day with 30 students in each class. By the end of the week, the teacher would have the opportunity to build relationships with 750 students within that week. The teacher has fifty minutes for each class: forty-eight minutes to teach per class, one minute to greet the students, and one minute to say goodbye to their students as they exit the classroom. The teacher has opportunities to reach 13,500 students each semester and 27,000 students in a year. With each contact, the teacher is building relationships and developing a mentorship with students.

Every Student Succeeds Act (ESSA) contributes to building relationships with students. ESSA works in schools in three areas: academics, attendance, and behavior. Increasing literacy skills of students will not only help the entire school but especially the students that read below grade level. This underdeveloped skill presents problems not only in English class but in math, science, and social studies. Reading comprehension and fluency are also affected. A strategic reading course helps students increase their reading level.

Attendance presents additional problems in schools. There are many reasons why students miss school; however, districts can directly affect their students' attendance by using data to identify and support students who may need extra support and services. Districts can use targeted supports to get students to school every day. Schools could notify the parent or guardian of student absence; develop and implement an absence intervention plan (which may include supportive services for students and families); offer counseling; provide parent education and parenting programs; offer mediation or intervention programs available through juvenile authorities; and as a last resort, if applicable, schools could file truancy. Schools can also monitor students' behavior using levels I and II modifications. Level I modifications are goal setting, student handbook, freshman seminar (social skills), report card conferences, adult mentors, assemblies/rallies, climate chart (restorative justice practices), days of peace, data walls, dollars system, positive notes home, PBIS, student of the month, and uniform incentives. Level II modifications include behavior plans, lunch detention, one-on-one meetings with the student, seat changes, buddy classrooms, coach/advisor/mentor follow-up, peer mediation, student mentoring with a teacher team, after-school programs, mentoring, peace circles, contracts, daily reports, phone calls home, and parent-teacher conferences.

Educators should know that building relationships with students will earn trust and respect. Students respond positively when teachers help them feel safe. It is essential that teachers' personal issues do not interfere with building relationships with students. If the teacher is positive, the students will generally be positive. Talk to students about their interests and extracurricular activities. Take an interest in their interests even if you do not share the same passion. Teachers can attend ball games or extracurricular activities to show their support. Encourage your students to take their passions and interests and turn them into a career. Some teachers provide extra tutoring on their own time before and after school. Some teachers donate clothing, shoes, food, or other household goods that a family needs to survive. The focus of building relationships with students is recognizing student needs inside and outside the classroom and assisting in meeting those needs.

Students will never respect the teacher if the teacher does not respect them. Teachers should not yell, use sarcasm, single a student out, or attempt to embarrass a student. Those things will lead to a loss of respect. Teachers should handle situations professionally. Teachers must treat each student the same. The same set of rules must apply to all students. It is also vital that a teacher is fair and consistent when dealing with students.

Building relationships with 150 students per day will help to reverse underachievement and low achievement among students in urban schools. Some people ask, "Isn't that what teachers do every day?" But obviously it is not that simple, because if it was, America's education system would not continue to create inequalities. School districts, administration, teachers, staff, students, and parents should work together to build community in school. Community can be used in many ways (e.g., community in schools, community learning, and community partners). Community in schools involves ways to better educate and prepare students for civic, political, individual, and community welfare concerns. Building relationships and community in the classroom are important goals that I learned from years of teaching.

CHAPTER 2
PHILOSOPHIES OF EDUCATION

Teaching philosophies are broken into categories of thought. The three categories are reality, knowledge, and values. The system works as a machine because each main category has subparts. Reality is divided into metaphysics (the mind and eternal ideas), ontology, and cosmology. Knowledge is divided into epistemology (a rational body of truth) of scientific inquiry and reasoning. Values are divided into axiology (absolute eternal reflection of God) of ethics and aesthetics.

Teaching is often faced with controversial issues. For example, should moral education, charter education, or values education be a responsibility of the school? Ideas and answers to this question date back to Western philosophers and philosophies like Neo-Thomism, Greece, and Plato. Rene Descartes, Immanuel Kant, and Dewey are philosophers who founded ideas of education based on realism, pragmatism, and existentialism. These theories provide meaning to the purpose of education, curriculum, and instruction. Eastern philosophies such as Hinduism, Buddhism, Confucianism, and Taoism are influenced by religious thought, absolute truths, and the journey of oneself. Western philosophies, however, somewhat tend to ignore religious influences. The foundation of education is a combination of traditional and contemporary philosophies.

Educational theory has grown throughout centuries. The purpose of schooling and the nature of the learner connect to curriculum and instructional methods. The teacher manages the classroom using several proponents and theories of education. The six areas of educational theory are perennialism, progressivism, behaviorism, essentialism, reconstructionism, and postmodernism.

Perennialism theory follows teaching truth and intellect and developing spiritual nature to prepare for life. Students learn about value, worth, Christianity, liberal arts, fine arts, and moral development. Teachers use the coaching method, critical thinking, and questioning techniques. Leading theorists are Jacques Maritian, Robert Hutchins, Mortimer Adler, and Allan Bloom.

The progressivism model follows the democratic process and encourages cooperation and decision-making in lesson planning. The students learn by doing, interacting with the environment, and experiencing testing and evaluation. The curriculum is reflective, child centered, and community centered. Instruction includes projects, critical thinking, problem-solving, and cooperative learning. There are formative assessments with the teacher monitoring and ongoing feedback. Francis Parker, John Dewey, Ella Flagg-Young, and William Kilpatrick are leading proponents of this model.

Ivan Pavlor, John Watson, E. L. Thorndike, B. F. Skinner, and David Premack were leaders in the behaviorism model. This model reinforces appropriate behavior and uses a curriculum of individualized cognitive problem-solving. Instructional methods are classical and operant conditioning. Teachers who use this method are skilled in technical and observational skills and trained in educational psychology.

Essentialism is a model that teaches about culture and traditions. Instruction is focused on oral and written communication. The teachers are trained in liberal arts, sciences, and humanities. William Bagley, Arthur Bestor, and Diane Ravitch are some of the leading theorists.

Cynthia Price

The reconstructionism model examines education reform. The teacher is a shaper of new ideas, change, transformational leader, and community advocate. Karl Marx and Paulo Freire are leading proponents of this model.

The postmodernism model follows cultural politics that challenge all unequal power. Instructional methods examine autobiographical histories, languages and cultures. Leading researchers are Michael Apple, Michael Foucault, and Henry Giroux.

American Education: European Heritage and Colonial Experience

America has developed its educational system based on influences from China, Egypt, and Greece. China's influence focuses on cultural heritage in order to develop the moral person that knows how to solve problems of society and government. Egypt teachings were connected to the temple and taught writing, math, and science. Greece focused on the young and used principals of city-states.

Philosophies of Socrates, Plato, and Aristotle were known for dialectical teaching, lecture method, and scientific methods. The Romans are credited for the grammar school, the importance of play and relaxation in western education. The concept of liberal education, Socratic, and scientific methods were derived from Athens. These concepts in education were discovered in the Middle Ages. The Renaissance followed and the liberal arts played a huge factor during this time period. Curriculum included grammar, logic, rhetoric, arithmetic, geometry, astronomy, and music. The Reformation period relied on religion with the teaching of Martin Luther, John Calvin, and the Vernacular Schools. Other influences in European educational thought were Francis Bacon, John Locke, and Jean-Jacques Rousseau.

Education in Colonial America was experienced through the Natives and Puritans cultures. The Native American tribes had three main points which were economic survival skills, knowledge of cultural heritage, and spiritual awareness. The Puritans had a religious and literacy focus. The Calvin's view of education centered on the dame school held in kitchens and living rooms. Education became more advanced for secondary and university students.

As society changed through economic and social advances the colonies became more independent. Benjamin Franklin influenced academy schools and Latin grammar schools. High school education became important after the Revolutionary War and the College of William and Mary was established in 1693.

American Education: From Revolution to the Twentieth Century
July 4, 1776 was the day that America became the land of the free and essential nationalism became a part of the education system. Laws for the educational system detailed public over private interests. The creation of independent citizenship, improvement of human conditions, and liberty of learning were the focus of America's educational system.

Key names like Thomas Jefferson, Benjamin Rush, and Noah Webster were founders of innovative schools. Monitorial, Charity, and Sunday schools were formed by 1830 and Academy Schools followed with the concept of practical education with a traditional curriculum. Changes in education took place in 1830-1860 because people moved to cities. The Common School Movement began and demands of the working class forced the educational system to change. During the time leading people in education were Horace Mann, Henry Barnard, and Catharine. The states supported the schools and school boards and school districts were formed. Education became compulsory and a movement of higher education became the focus of America's educational system.

Equal education for minorities created dissonances in America's educational system. Arguments about educating minorities date back to Booker T. Washington, W.E.B. Dubois, and the famous case *Plessy v Ferguson*. America has endured through its hardships of the education system and today schools are integrated. For the most part schools are rebuilding and producing productive citizens.

Formal training for teachers began to thrive and the term "career teachers" was recognized. Teacher institutes were developed and curriculum and standards were strengthened.

CHAPTER 3

MODERN AMERICAN EDUCATION: FROM THE PROGRESSIVE MOVEMENT TO THE PRESENT

America's educational system is affected by people, population growth, cultures, politics and policies. Schools operations are determined by enrollment, attendance, instructional staff, finances, and funding. These factors continue to evolve over the years beginning with the John Hopkins University Child Study in 1884. This study focused on the importance of cognitive development in children. Another known study is the development of Intelligence Quotient (IQ) which studied the emotional growth and personality development of children.

The Great Depression had a serious impact on the operations of schools. Teachers were unable to be paid, class size increased, curriculum was cut, and teachers were cut. President Roosevelt created The New Deal which provided relief for the schools. Many programs were developed and The Public Works Administration (PWA) provided assistance to public buildings and schools. The Bureau of Indian Affairs was created to help the plight of the Native American. The post war years brought the GI Bill of Rights. The Montessori Movement increased in 1950 and Head Start Programs were created.

After the Sputnik curriculum expanded to vocational and factory education. Several programs were created to bring awareness to the War on Poverty. The Civil Rights Movement also affected the educational system. Brown v. Board of Education of Topeka (1954) court case prevented segregated schools. The 1968 Bilingual Education Act increased funding for districts with low income students with limited English proficiency. In 2000 the No Child Left Behind bill was implemented and charter schools and school choice increased. The latest school reform is Obama's Race to the Top (RTT) plan.

Development of the Teaching Profession

Education is essential to any society. Thomas Jefferson wrote "If a nation expects to be ignorant and free in a state of civilization, it expects what never was and never will be." This quote expresses the importance of education to every society. Teachers are the foundation of every society and throughout history teachers have been regulated and monitored. The teaching profession is an important profession and is regulated by a code of professional standards and ethics. The Interstate New Teacher Assessment and Support Consortium (INTASC) are examples of professional standards. Professionalization of teaching has increased through the years.

There are many different ways for a teacher to exercise professionalism. Teachers can obtain a National Board Certificate, attend professional development, engage in action research, and participate in mentoring programs. Teachers can join special groups for example Council for Exceptional Children (CEC) and National Conference of Teachers of English (NCTE) to increase their professionalism. There are many groups that advocate for teachers. The National Education Association, American Federation of Teachers, and many more state affiliations offer teacher support, professional development, and advocacy. Teaching organizations support teachers and help teachers negotiate teaching contracts. These agencies also have assisted in elevating teaching as a profession.

Teachers are responsible for license renewal and have opportunities for career advancement. Opportunities range from specialized knowledge in Advance Placement (AP) training, preparation of curriculum, and multiple career paths such as teacher leader or curriculum leader. Teachers have autonomy within the profession and are evaluated by performance systems such as Value Added and Annually Year Progress (AYP). These systems monitor student's yearly progress according to what the student has learned.

Teaching as a Profession

The status of the teaching profession is positive for teachers who are full of energy and are willing to try new ideas in the classroom. In 2019, 71.2% of teachers were female and 80% were white. This statistic presents a problem because America's student population is increasing, are minority and marginalized therefore the need for diverse teaching methods are in high demand. Novice teachers have to develop a diverse toolbox and experiences in order to be successful in the classroom. The reasons why one may become a teacher vary, but one assumption that seems to remain true, is that teachers make differences in the students' lives, whether the child is in elementary, middle, or high school.

America has surpassed the classical education system. There are a number of educational programs for all types of students. However, the structure of the system basically remains the same regardless if it is elementary, middle, or high school. Teacher education programs and licensing requirements vary depending on the program. Teachers are required to be highly qualified and there are rigorous standards to monitor the profession. The NCATE standards regulate the profession and requirements for teaching license range from the completion of BS, BA, and Praxis I-II. Each state has different requirements. There are alternative, emergency, and national certifications licensure.

Cynthia Price

There are two teacher perceivers used for interviewing teachers, Rural and Suburban districts use the standard teacher perceiver and Urban districts usually use the Urban teacher perceiver. Rottier, Kelly, and Tomhave found that many teachers in rural schools experience personal teaching dissatisfaction. Specific concerns were related to unhappiness with the community, administration and expectations for teachers. A variety of studies on urban teachers' problems and stresses indicate that their areas of dissatisfaction are more often related to physical harassment, large classes, and lack of close relationships with students. Salaries for teachers vary depending on certifications', district (urban, suburban, and rural). experiences, supply and demand, and supplemental pay. Indirect compensation and employee benefits and services vary according to district, union, or placement.

CHAPTER 4

THE SOCIAL AND CULTURAL CONTEXTS OF SCHOOLING

The relationship of school and society changed and schools became socialization agents. Family structure, peer groups, media, culture and religion changed the dynamics of schools and community. The purpose and expectation of schools served as functionalist, conflict and symbolic perspectives. The concept of social class or socioeconomic status (SES) rapidly developed throughout the educational system and ideas of inequality surface in schools.

The social class achievement and attainment gaps presented problems for school systems. Minorities performed lower on achievement tests than their white counterparts and standardized testing became a controversial issue. Issues of racial and ethnic achievement and attainment gaps greatly increased which caused great concerns with reading and math standardized tests. Minorities performed significantly lower followed by high school matriculation rates were lower for African and Hispanics students.

The Individuals with Disabilities Education Act (IDEA) provided educational opportunities for children with learning, visual, emotional, deaf, blindness, and autism disabilities. The deficit-hyperactivity disorder

(ADHA) is not covered under IDEA however this disorder is present in almost every classroom. With this being said many classrooms across America have a large number of unidentified special education students who are not receiving proper services in the educational system.

Responding to Diversity

Multicultural education provides many opportunities for students in schools. For example Multicultural literature helps students connect their experiences and book's events to everyday life. One way to support multicultural education is to study histories, lullabies, nursery rhymes, ballads, songs, and folktales from different cultures. Often a traditional fairytale is retold across cultures and the original meaning is changed to reflect a specific culture. Whatever lesson is used to teach multiculturalism educators should examine literature to determine if it is an accurate representation of the culture it represents. Teachers need to use diverse literature to increase choice and opportunities for students in and outside the classroom. Students that enjoy reading as a child and into adulthood increase their chances for upward mobility in the educational system.

There is a demand to bring people together and increase contact, cultural interaction and conflict resolution. Culturally Responsive teaching is using standards, knowledge, and skills to teach students that are expected to learn dominant culture pedagogy. Teachers can use culturally responsive techniques to accomplish academic outcomes, meet the standards of reading different materials for a variety of purposes, and understand the meaning of what is read. The technique connects theory ideas of culture to other subject's skills, and domains of interest in the educational setting making both instructional content and technique connections. Examples of culturally responsive teaching are promoting social justice for ethnically diverse groups that connect to civil rights protests in social studies, contemporary song lyrics for music appreciation classes, paintings of different ethnic artists to illustrate artistic techniques, and ethnic political rhetoric. Social commentary poetry in language arts and literature classes are also considered culturally teaching.

Children with exceptional needs present other challenges in inclusion and diversity. The Individuals with Disabilities Education Act (IDEA) is a 1975 law enacted by Congress that defines strict guidelines for states to follow in order to get funding for special education. The financial support for special education programs is granted on the condition that districts make available to every student with special educational needs a "free appropriate public education," provided "to the maximum extent appropriate" in the "least restrictive environment." School districts must work with the parents to develop and implement a successful educational placement. If necessary the educator must be ready to consider full regular education classrooms as a placement of the child. Cultural reconstruction is needed so inclusive education is moved beyond assimilation.

Students at Risk and At-Risk Behavior

Students can become at-risk and teachers are trained to use interventions in the classroom to help students overcome this category. Some teachers have Early Warning Indicators (EWI) meetings to talk about how to help students with risk factors such as attendance, behaviors, and academics. These meetings help teachers create prevention and intervention strategies to help At -Risk youth. Some school districts have programs or school reform models that deal directly with At-Risk youth. For example, Diplomas Now identifies students early and works to eliminate the problems that lead to dropping out: poor attendance, poor behavior or course failure in English or math. The program also works with the collaboration of City Year, an AmeriCorps program that unites diverse young leaders for a year of full-time service (Diplomas Now). City Year corps members are trained to work in under-served schools to provide targeted academic and school-wide interventions to help students get on track and stay on track to graduate.

Students are also At-Risk if they are physically, sexually, or emotionally abused. Teachers are mandated reporters so when teachers discover any abuse occurring they must report the signs to children services. School violence is another reason why students are considered At-Risk. Peer harassment, fighting, and weapons put students At- Risk. Schools should have health professionals on site to help students through challenging times. Prevention and Intervention programs will strengthen protective factors for At-Risk students.

CHAPTER 5

DIVERSITY IN SCHOOLS

An important fact about cultural identity is that shared information about understanding of diversity, equity, and equality with colleagues will help create a safe space for diversity and inclusion in the schools. I learned that all three components affect a student's achievement. I gained insight on diversity and equity programs that districts and teachers used to support general education ELL, ELA and Special education students.

These topics impose barriers for social change in schools. The question of how educational goods should be equitably distributed remains a controversial topic. I believe the research of Bourdieu's work focuses on cultural capital networks available and used by schools. Increased cultural and social capitals in schools, depends on students learning standards, norms, values, and beliefs that help students navigate successfully through the educational system. These norms are help agents and coping strategies in society. Cultural capital is effectively transmitted within the family and depends on the quantity and quality of cultural capital accumulated. The more social and cultural capitals are prevented from being transferred the circle of inequalities continues in schools.

There are many cultures represented in my school African American, Bi-racial, White, Somali, Nepali, African, and Latino. Most students live in the surrounding area of the school. The school supports the community and the community supports the school. However, this is not the case in all schools in the district. I have recently reviewed an article called *White Teachers in Urban Classrooms: Embracing Non-White Students' Cultural Capital for Better Teaching and Learning* by Barry M. Goldenberg. This article gives some bold facts about teachers teaching students of color. The cultural aspects are examined through this reading and discusses some hard truths about education. For example, by 2050 almost two thirds of all American children are projected to be students of color. 63 of the 100 largest U.S. school districts are already more than half students of color. "The clash of cultures often occurs inside classrooms between students of color from mostly low-income households and their teachers who are predominantly White and middle class." (Goldenberg) These facts create a clear picture of cultural diversity in America, but the teaching profession reflects a different picture.

The article suggests a **"call to action"** for White teachers in urban classrooms to rethink non-White students' cultural capital in the context of teaching and learning. Educators should not "ignore that students should and can possess different kinds of cultural capital"—in what Carter refers to as "non-dominant" cultural capital (Carter, 2005, p. 10). It is the responsibility of the teacher to recognize this capital and pedagogically utilize it in the classroom in ways that enhance student learning (Goldenberg).

There have been many opportunities over the years that I have extended support to colleagues. Most recently these opportunities involve mentor to new teachers for Diplomas Now Model, ELA AIR Advisory committee member, developed curriculum for Strategic Reading Course, served on committees in building TBT and EWI meetings, Co- teacher for (ELL and Special Education) ninth grade English and Strategic Reading students, and collected assessment data (SLO) for English 9 co-taught class.

I look for opportunities to grow in and outside of my classroom and develop culturally responsive pedagogy. I have developed a reform plan called (150 50 Project). My plan involves presenting research about how to monitor students to achieve success. The plan is a qualitative action research case study (QUAL-quan) method. I have taken time to listen and give advice to colleagues in need. I mentor new teachers and work with administrators to solve problems.

CHAPTER 6
"RACIAL AND ETHNIC ACHIEVEMENT GAPS"

The "achievement gap" in education refers to the disparity in academic performance between groups of students. The achievement gap shows up in grades, standardized-test scores, course selection, and dropout rates. The Stanford Center for Educational Policy and Analysis reports progress has been made in improving racial educational disparities in schools. But that progress has been slow, uneven, and incomplete (Stanford).

Sample students around the United States between the ages of 9,13, and 17 were given tests in math and reading as a part of the National Assessment of Educational Progress, sometimes called "The Nation's Report Card". These tests provided the public and policymakers with information to frame policies that will help to narrow the racial gap. The test is reliable and the research dates back to 1970's.

The research used QUAN- qual – Inferential Statistics Standard Deviation 0.5 to 0.9 -– Stanford University- The Educational Opportunity Monitoring Project. The research design was Correlational -The National Assessment of Educational Progress (NAEP). NAEP, sometimes called "The Nation's Report Card," which is designed to provide the public and policymakers with an objective assessment of the math and reading skills of American children. NAEP examines trends in the white-black and white-Hispanic achievement gaps using math and reading skills.

The NAEP tests in math and reading were used to determine the narrowing factor of achievement gaps for Black and Hispanic students. The average 9-year-old student today scores almost as well on the NAEP math tests as the average 13-year-old did in 1978; the average 13-year-old scores almost as well as the average 17-year-old in 1978. The scores from the NAEP tests were taken from state to state. The researchers sampled students using the Main NAEP every two years since 2003. The study exhibited graphs charting the results of the research findings.

Black and Hispanic students are roughly three years ahead of their parents' generation in math skills. In reading, they are roughly two to three years ahead of their parents. White students' scores have also improved, but not by as much. The findings revealed that White-black and white-Hispanic achievement gaps have narrowed substantially since the 1970s in all grades and in both math and reading. The study shows that some of the achievement gaps grew larger in the late 1980s and the 1990s. As of 2012, the white-black and white -Hispanic achievement gaps were 30-40% smaller than they were in the 1970s. The study shows that over the past 40 years, white-black and white -Hispanic achievement gaps have been declining. Black and Hispanic students today are about three years ahead of their parents' generation in math skills. In reading, they are roughly two to three years ahead of their parents.

Achievement gaps vary from state to state. The researchers sampled students using the Main NAEP every two years since 2003. The Midwest states data determined the white-black achievement gap has generally been larger than a standard deviation over the last decade, regardless of grade or subject. In Connecticut, Nebraska and the District of Columbia the gap is well over 1.5 standard deviations. The same is true of the white-Hispanic achievement gaps. In some states New England, Connecticut, Massachusetts, and Rhode Island the achievement gap ranges, on the order of 0.90 to 1.00 standard deviations. Each state varies as to why the achievement gaps are large but the findings support large gaps are due to white students that score particularly high on the NAEP tests; in other cases, the gaps are large because black or Hispanic students score poorly.

The racial and ethnic achievement gaps that exist in schools raises issues in the battle of equal education for all students. Educational inequality with minorities has a history in the United States dated back to slavery. Plessy v. Ferguson (1892) "separate but equal" doctrine created educational disparities in schools and later was overturned in a Supreme Court ruling of Brown v. Board of Education (1954). One measure of racial educational equality are racial achievement gaps that differ in standardized test scores of white and black or white and Hispanic students. Achievement gaps are one way of monitoring the equality of educational outcomes. Another measure is researching the state's racial socioeconomic make-up.

The goal of the research is to alert the Nation to the critical state of the educational system. One means to improve lies in decreasing the achievement gaps between African-American and Hispanic students. Standardized testing is a law in Ohio and has become a tool for measuring performance of students, schools and teachers. Testing has become the basis for state grades for schools and are used to make policy and used to evaluate school performance. It has been argued that standardized testing lacks equity for all students. The study was retrospective using inferential statistics and the NAEP math and reading tests are reliable sources nationwide. Achievement gaps are strongly correlated with racial gaps in income, poverty rates, unemployment rates, and educational attainment. Higher-income and more-educated families can provide more educational opportunities for their children, and family socioeconomic resources are strongly related to educational outcomes.

According to the article racial socioeconomic disparity is a very good predictor of its racial achievement gap, some states with similar levels of socioeconomic disparities have substantially different achievement gaps. For example, New Jersey and Wisconsin have very similar (and very high) levels of white-black socioeconomic disparities, but the white-black math achievement gap in Wisconsin is considerably larger (roughly 0.25 standard deviations larger) than in New Jersey. This suggests that socioeconomic disparities are not the sole cause of racial achievement gaps. Other factors—including potentially the availability and quality of early childhood education, the quality of public schools, patterns of residential and school segregation, and state educational and social policies—may play important roles in reducing or exacerbating racial achievement gaps. The article explained the procedures of the NAEP tests (math and reading) and the correlational factors. The article had an additional section that explained the Educational Opportunity Monitoring Project focus was on two dimensions of educational equity: patterns of *educational opportunity and experiences* and patterns of *educational progress and outcomes*. *Educational progress and outcomes* include early childhood development and school readiness; academic performance and proficiency; social, emotional, and behavioral development; and educational progress and attainment, including high school graduation, college enrollment, and college completion. Using the best available data, the Project monitors progress toward equality of these outcomes among students of different race/ethnicity, family socioeconomic background, and gender.

Educational opportunities and experiences include children's access to developmentally-appropriate and stimulating environments in early childhood; access to high-quality pre-schools, elementary schools, and high schools, staffed by skilled teachers; exposure to rigorous, expansive curricula; and affordable and useful college options. Educational opportunity can be difficult to measure, both because "school quality" is not simply defined or quantified and because the United States has not collected systematic data on the quality of education children have access to and receive. In lieu of ideal data on educational opportunity and experiences, the Project will document patterns and trends in a set of related features of education, including patterns of segregation, school funding, pupil-teacher ratios, and teacher characteristics.

Racial socioeconomic disparities are the primary explanation for racial achievement gaps, which means achievement gaps were largest in places where racial socioeconomic disparities are largest, and were expected to be zero in places where there is no racial socioeconomic inequality. State racial achievement gaps are strongly correlated with state racial socioeconomic disparities. One explanation for racial achievement gaps is due to socioeconomic disparities between white, black, and Hispanic families. Black and Hispanic children's parents typically have lower incomes and lower levels of educational attainment than white children's parents. These facts prove the necessary attainment of social and cultural capitals.

The finding suggests that socioeconomic disparities are not the sole cause of racial achievement gaps. Other factors that contribute to high achievement gaps are the variability and quality of early childhood education, the quality of public schools, patterns of residential and school segregation, and state educational and social policies may play important roles in reducing or exacerbating racial achievement gaps.

CHAPTER 7

ONLINE LEARNING

Virtual learning K 12 presents challenges for students because students may not have the motivation and structure to be consistent in the online learning format. Students need guidance and face to face contact and instruction. In theory, the process sounds like it will work. However, online schooling could present many problems for students. These problems consist of time management, motivation, skill level, and technology use. Some students do not have the technology in their home to carry out the assignments.

Students have interactions, teaching, learning, and social interactions in a traditional school setting. Teachers in suburban, rural and urban settings agree that students generally perform better with face to face teaching. Research claimed that by 2019 50% of all courses and grades 9 through 12 will be delivered online. The COVID pandemic supports research. This fact is very scary for teachers. Some students were not prepared to follow the criteria and demands of online learning. When students returned to school after COVID students were deficient in reading, writing, math skills.

Additional arguments in education present issues with the point that public setting has to take all students regardless of behavior, grade level, and skill sets. I would argue the point *"students leave traditional public school for virtual school so parents could have more support at home. They wanted their elder child to be at home to help take care of younger siblings or help around the home."* I am not so sure this is the case for Urban students. Typically students leave for more freedom from a structured setting, or work a job to support as added income to the family. I would argue questions centered around how successful would English Language Learners, Learning Disabilities and Emotionally disturbed students be with processes of online learning?

America's education system already feeds into the school to prison pipeline, just imagine the cost of for profit prisons would sky rocket. Online learning also presents equity issues in education, not to mention the ECOT situation which occurred in Columbus, Ohio where 80 million dollars was mismanaged. This situation left a huge deficiency in Ohio's education system. Personally I think online learning presents challenges in K-12 education. To some this phrase may be extreme however I am left with Kurtz's dying words in the book "The Heart of Darkness "The horror! The horror!"

Interdisciplinary Tech-integration

Technology integration is a major factor in the daily operations of schools. Teachers need to be well versed in technology success, objectives and timeline of projects success criteria listed in the building. Every school should have a technology network diagram which shows the logical flow of technology plans in the building. One way to accomplish this step is to consider interests, skills and experience. people in the building that choose to be involved in technology planning. This step will help the school's tech plan to be successful. Personalized stake in the plan will allow leaders to emerge in the e-learning community. Educational technologies would change how learning is organized and supported in the technology project. The success of the project would influence positive e-learning changes in each department. All departments would have a stake in the project, and perhaps the project could be showcased in individual schools.

A technology coach in the building could provide opportunities for teachers. The coach's role could be data collector for departments, school attendance, and technology lesson planning. The tech coach could also create a discussion circle for teachers to initiate technology instruction. A technology coach could be very beneficial to teachers.Experts suggest that coaching improves instruction. Trust must be formed and coaches must know what effective teaching looks like. One important role of a coach is building relationships with teachers. A coach provides advice to improve instruction.A coach needs the trust of the teacher. A coach provides researched based learner-centered strategies.

Professional development is essential for technology coaches and teachers. One step could include teachers meeting in groups on various topics related to schools technology needs. Teachers receive credit for attending the PD. Technology sessions could include reading,hands-on activities and shared learning experience. These principles might be applied when functioning as a technology coach for teachers. Some teachers might have a lot of experience using various software packages while others might be new to using software packages for learning and teaching. Also, a coach should keep in mind that the teacher is the subject matter expert and would know best how the technology might be used to enhance the learning experience for their students. Keeping the experience of the teacher in mind would greatly affect the outcomes of goal setting. The teacher knows best about the workings of their classroom. E-coaching and live coaching are effective techniques, but correcting and giving suggestions in front of students in a live setting or with an earpiece in most cases is not effective.

In a recent study a teacher commented "I have worked in a lot of different environments besides teaching. In every situation, I had to go through on the job training where a supervisor demonstrated and instructed the necessary skills to complete the task. But as an educator short of a "professional semester" in college I was thrown to 150+ students with limited skills and expected to teach them. The workforce is much better structured for the adult learner than the field of education. As I think back on the many PD sessions that I have lived through as a teacher, there are few clear differences between the good and back sessions. As a science teacher, the PD was very department driven. The group of science teachers chose the problem areas to focus on and created the path we wanted to go to better the learning experience and outcomes for our students." The Techin' Ain't Easy group offered some great self-discoveries in regards to "I didn't know that" about coaching educators. The Knowles principle certainly brings a teacher to a point of clarity where a teacher cannot teach/coach other adults as they teach children."

It has been suggested that adults learners learn best under the following circumstances:

1. The learning is self-directed.
2. The learning is experiential and utilizes background knowledge.
3. The learning is relevant to current roles.
4. The instruction is problem-centered.
5. The students are motivated to learn.

The above suggestions may not apply to all adult learners, however education research has proven that students learn differently according to age, learning environment, literacy, and learning opportunities.

The Technological Pedagogical Content Knowledge Framework (TPACK) is a system put in place to help students and teachers to understand the format and illustrations implemented in technology usage.The TPACK model provides guidelines to help teachers with technology integration in the classroom. Real world application, instructional delivery and visuals are included in the instructional packet. Teachers have commented that real-life examples create connections between the content of the model and actual technology integration efforts created by the teacher and student. The model uses news stories and students create notes from the assignment article on a topic that they have researched. The interconnectedness of the model is what makes the model work. The technological, pedagogical, and content knowledge overlap with content and social presence of learners. Students project their personal characteristics into the community of inquiry, thereby presenting themselves as 'real people.'

The cognitive presence is the extent to which the participants in any particular configuration of a community of inquiry are able to construct meaning through sustained communication. The teacher designs instructional materials, create the course online using effective learning and design strategies.Teaching presence is defined as the design, facilitation, and direction of cognitive and social processes for the purpose of realizing personally meaningful and educational worthwhile learning outcomes. Students online, interact with teaching content, classroom attendance monitoring, and course management. The teacher is the course facilitator and provides support for the student within the virtual school.

The teacher collaborates with students to construct online courses.The teacher is the mentor and advocate for students.The teacher assists students in registering and accessing virtual courses and provides academic tutoring and assistance to students.Teachers have commented positively and some have challenges with the use of TPACK. The pedagogical information in the program is great however the program presents challenges with novice technology users.The model is informative and teachers were to be introduced to the model. The video helped explain concepts in the model.

Social Presence:

The video allowed students to express their viewpoints on the slide. I felt the teacher did too much lecturing. I was easily distracted so I am sure the students were distracted during the lecture. A video clip would create a break for visual learners.

Cognitive presence:

Some of the slides were confusing, and wordy. The color of the back ground and the font size made some slides appear to be information overload. The images fit each slide but sometimes the images were distracting.

Teaching presence:

I saw and heard the teacher explaining points before, during and after each slide. The teacher gave points about what was going to be on the OGT Social Studies Test. I think the lecture was helpful but it was too long. I am sure students may have watched the lecture in two parts.

I see that people are excited about K 12 virtual schools, but I am concerned because students may not have the motivation and structure to be consistent in online learning courses. Secondary students need guidance and face to face contact with an instructor. In theory, the process sounds like it will work. However, online schooling could present many problems for students. These problems consist of time management, motivation, skill level, and technology use. Some students do not have the technology in their home to carry out the assignments.

I have worked in an Urban education setting for 30 years and many of the students that I teach (or have taught) have been successful because of the interactions, teaching, learning, and social interactions in a traditional school setting. I have also taught in a rural setting and I also think students in this setting need similar teaching and learning experiences as students in an Urban setting.

According to the reading by 2019 there is a possibility that 50% of all courses and grades 9 through 12 will be delivered in online settings. This fact is very scary for me as a teacher. I am not worried about my job, but I am worried about students who are not capable of following the criteria of online learning.

CHAPTER 8

DIVERSITY IN ONLINE TEACHING

Diversity in online teaching is a trending topic in the 21st century. Teachers use a tremendous amount of online visuals to attract the attention of their students. The phone, chrome book, Ipad, laptop, desktop computer and other devices are essential components to virtual teaching. The Interaction Institute for Social Change (IISC) brings much to the table when teaching about Social Justice and racial equity. Their mission is to build collaborative capacity in individuals, organizations, and networks working toward Social Justice and racial equity. The organization started in 1993 to collaborate with the social sector through thousands of individuals, and hundreds of organizations and networks working to advance social justice. Over time they have focued on the profound and persistent racial inequities that destroy people, communities, and the planet. Guided by our values and Collaborative Change Lens, their approach to supporting individuals, organizations, and networks to shift systems so that groups and communities that have been historically marginalized and oppressed by racism and other isms have an equitable share in the power and control of organizational and societal resources in order to ensure they are able to thrive and contribute to their communities and organizations.

Richard Williams, better known by the name Prince EA, is an American rapper, spoken word artist, music video director and rights activist from St Louis, Missouri. His youtube channel goal is to make people laugh, cry, think, and love with the ultimate goal to evolve. This resource has inspiring videos that speak many truths about educational truths. The video *Where fish are no longer forced to climb trees* describes how America's educational system creates unequal schools. Teachers use these resources to differentiate instruction in areas such as content, product or process. Teachers also present materials in various formats, lecture, small groups, collaborative projects, individualized work. Teachers use technology to meet the needs of all learners.

Technology enables educators to tailor content and assessments for individual learners and allow students to be more creative using multimedia presentations. Teachers use technology for knowledge checks and provide advanced or remedial content. One example used to increase reading comprehension is Newsela. Newsela allows students to read current events articles and then allows the teacher to scale reading levels based on short cycle assessments. Google apps foster collaboration and peer editing. Teachers and students can work on the same document and comment with editing suggestions.Teachers can group students and give individualized assignments.

Blended learning refers to situations where students receive instruction in both face-to-face and online environments. Embedded within the concept is an assumption that blended learning environments also give students some control over the pace, flow or focus of their schoolwork, which aligns blended learning to the student empowerment at the heart of the 2016 ISTE Standards for Students. Blended learning includes classrooms that have been fully "flipped," as well as the many that take a more hybrid and varied approach. Teachers use a variety of reference guides to help students to complete technology projects.

Redefining learning in a technology-driven world

The ISTE Standards are about pedagogy, not tools. Which is to say, they emphasize the ways that technology can be used to transform learning and teaching.The potential for technology to mend gaps in equity, engage students as unique individuals and prepare them for an uncertain future. The ISTE Standards for Students embrace these challenges and envision shifts to education that support students as they become agentic, future focused and adaptable. ISTE's methodology has been collaborative, purposive and grounded. Empowering students to take ownership of their learning emerged as a major theme during the refresh.

Research indicates that empowering students to have agency in their education and lives leads to many positive outcomes, including that students do better in inequality of access situations, are able to personalize their learning and achieve regardless of ability and build dispositional skills, such as executive functioning, perseverance, self-awareness and tolerance for ambiguity, that many believe are necessary to thrive in current and future society.

Computational thinking

Being able to think and solve problems in the way that a computer is designed to solve problems is a vital skill in today's digital age. Computational thinking (CT) is a problem-solving process that includes but also exceeds coding. It is fundamental to solving problems via computer applications but its methods can be used in a variety of situations and approaches. CT combines logic and deep knowledge of the fundamentals of how computers "think." Thus it is an important, contemporary literacy for all students, not just those who are likely to become software engineers. Even if students do not pursue computing in their careers, they will need to be familiar with the vocabulary and processes to effectively communicate with colleagues on technical issues and to be knowledgeable themselves about how computing works and affects their lives.

ISTE has for several years been a thought leader in supporting computational thinking in the classroom and extends this leadership by the overt place CT holds in the 2016 student standards.

Social and emotional skills

Largely, the research into social and emotional skills is meant to switch the focus from the "self-esteem" movement that dominated in the 1990s and early 2000s to a more personalized and empowered approach.

Futurism in the contemporary context is a field of science and philosophy focused on predicting the future, often the near-future. This field influenced the ISTE Standards for Students refresh in two key ways. First, experts on work in the U.S. argue that working life in the future will look significantly different than it does now, and that many of today's students will be working in jobs that have not yet been invented. To put stakeholders in this future frame of mind when thinking about the next iteration of the ISTE Standards for Students, ISTE drew from the work of the Institute for the Future to challenge current understandings of the world of work and how education plays into it as well as to inspire new ideas. Second, ISTE also consulted the 2014 and 2015 NMC Horizon Reports, which report on trends and transitions in K-12 education and project their likely impact. These reports helped ISTE prioritize concepts, hone focus and inspire out-of-the-box thinking about the near-future of education in drafting the 2016 student standards.

ISTE drew from the work of the Institute for the Future to challenge current understandings of the world of work and how education plays into it as well as to inspire new ideas.

Curation means "to take charge of or organize, to pull together, sift through, select for presentation, to heal and to preserve" and has generally referred to work with physical artifacts in libraries or museums (Mihaildis & Cohen, 2013, n.p.). In the digital age, however, curation can no longer remain a specialized skill set due to the vast amounts of information available to any individual with internet access, and it is intimately interconnected with the acquisition, construction and demonstration of knowledge.

Design processes and the maker movement The "maker movement" has become a particularly buzzy trend in education and factors into a larger conversation rethinking education.

But the overarching re-visioning of education manifested in the maker movement includes other principles such as learning based on projects or solving problems, situations where students develop social and emotional skills and the opportunity for students to become deep critical thinkers, creative communicators and dynamic collaborators.

Global citizens Asserting the value of global citizenship is an argument that feels both perennial and dated. It is certainly not new and yet affirming it continues to seem necessary. From ISTE's perspective, the topic's importance arises from a couple of factors. First, technology enables meaningful connections in ways never seen before

Common Core, Next Generation Science and other content-area standards

More and more education leaders recognize the need to prepare students for the digital age and they reflect this reality in the learning standards they adopt for their schools, districts and states. New learning standards, such as the CCSS, the NGSS and other state and content-area standards, now embed technical skills, such as keyboarding or calculator use, into their frameworks. Furthermore, some go as far as integrating activities that require technology, such as the listening or blogging requirements of the ELA CCSS or the more holistic approach to engineering, sciences and human culture in the NGSS.

The ISTE Standards provide a support framework across the grades and for all subject areas that serve as a groundwork for what's possible in learning using technology.

National Education Technology Plan

The National Education Technology Plan (NETP), released at the end of 2015, lays out the vision of the U.S. Department of Education for the purpose and use of technology in American education. Several of the NETP's focus align well with the 2016 ISTE Standards for Students, and there are key areas where the standards support and expand upon the NETP vision.

The Future Ready program serves as a key component of the Department of Education's ConnectED initiative under President Barack Obama. Future Ready focuses specifically on superintendents' committing to setting and implementing a vision for districtwide connectivity. The ISTE Standards for Students, as well as the other ISTE Standards, take these systems-level visions to the actual classroom. For example, Standard 2, Digital Citizen, takes a future-focused approach to what students need to be safe, legal, ethical and engaged citizens in the digital space. The standards can also serve as a guide for what professional learning to choose to best amplify pedagogy. Last, in tandem with the ISTE Essential Conditions, the ISTE Standards support a holistic vision for technology adoption and a re-visioning of digital age learning that goes beyond devices and connectivity to get to the unfulfilled potential of technology to transform learning.

Open Educational Resources (OER) are less an initiative than a movement that spans education from kindergarten through college and beyond. That said, the movement has the backing of the Office of Education Technology under President Barack Obama, which has been hard at work engaging companies to offer OER and encouraging districts to put forth OER curriculum and tool initiatives

The differences between 2007 and 2016 student standards is: If your school already uses the 2007 standards, you are well on your way to addressing the 2016 ISTE Standards for Students. The following crosswalks are intended to support adoption and implementation of the 2016 standards. The charts are intended to help identify where there are changes, advancements, new concepts or skills that have been eliminated. They are not intended to fully explain or describe the similarities and differences in the two sets of standards and in most cases, the correlations are partial or conceptual.

CHAPTER 9

STATE MANDATED TESTING
AN ERA OF CHANGE

I plan to examine The Ohio Department of Education Testing policies through the lens of equity. My research will include information from Ohio Department of Education, Political Education (Cross), Democratic Education (Gutmann), Seeking Common Ground (Tyack), Policy Paradox (Stone), the article State Mandated Testing and Educational Reform: Context and Consequences (Airasian), and additional findings about testing and student achievement.

Testing policy problems in Ohio are standardized testing is a law and has become a tool for measuring performance of students, schools and teachers. Testing has become the basis for state grades for schools and are used to make policy and used to evaluate school performance. The other side of the picture is testing presents an inaccurate picture and schools should focus on teaching students life skills. It has been argued that standardized testing lacks equity for all students. The recent policy about testing does not allow accommodations for limited language learners and special education students. The amount of time spent on testing is a question that policy makers need to consider. Does the test align to Common Core standards? Does the policy on testing consider equity? Does the testing policy consider students' learning objectives?

I plan to examine both sides of the issue using a democratic lens of education. I will also research the history of testing in Ohio, explain future plans for test implementation, and address possible questions that educators have about the new Language Arts test and provider the American Institute Research (ARI) which later developed in Ohio State Testing (OST). I also plan to present alternatives to the policy. I will provide evidence of how literacy is a very important part of testing and student learning objectives.

History of State Mandated Testing

The 1987 article *State Mandated Testing and Educational Reform: Context and Consequences* examine the debate over mandated testing and policy. This debate, as it did twenty-eight years ago, still exist in today's educational system. Peter W. Airasian the author of the article writes "that standardized tests are scientific and numerically scores are fair because all students are required to take and pass the identical test (Airasian)." This statement may be empirically true back in 1987 however drastic measures need to be taken when considering today's aggressive testing system. Mandated testing is referred to as high stakes tests. Today testing mandates control of our schools and presents unfair conditions for students. With the demands of testing given today I ask the same questions that the author asks: What attributes ought to be decisive in determining the distribution of educational resources to pupils? What factors ought to be decisive in determining whether a particular distribution of educational benefits is fair or unfair? Should academic, social, or personal goals take precedence in the schools and which goals within a selected category (Airasian)?

The educational system has changed since this article was written. The cost of education has increased in pupil ratio, graduation requirements have changed, standards have increased, and schools are now required to make available a social services network to students and parents. Schools are affected by decisions made at the federal and state levels about teaching, testing, curriculum, instruction, certification, funding, and evaluation. Politicians and interest groups have their agenda for the schools and often control decisions that affect educational practices and priorities. Ohio standardized testing policies were documented in the late 80's. In March 1987 The State Board of Education adopted a resolution recommending that the General Assembly enact legislation to require students to pass proficiency tests in order to graduate from high school (Trent).

> July the 117th General Assembly enacted H.B. 231 requiring anyone graduating in 1994 or thereafter to pass ninth grade proficiency tests in reading, writing, mathematics, and citizenship. This legislation also provided for twelfth grade proficiency tests in the same four areas that students would be required to pass to earn either the Diploma with Distinction or Diploma with Commendation (Trent).

> The 119th General Assembly in March 1992 enacted H.B. 55 which eliminated the Certificate of Attendance that was to be awarded to anyone who met all curriculum requirements but failed to pass the ninth grade tests and the Diplomas with Distinction and Commendation; retained the twelfth grade proficiency tests but prohibited requiring passage of these tests to earn the newly established Diploma with Honors; established proficiency testing in the same four areas at fourth and sixth grades beginning in 1994-95 and 1995-96, respectively; and added science tests at all four grades beginning in 1995-96 (Trent).

In July 1993-- The 120th General Assembly enacted H.B. 152, permitted districts to administer the ninth grade tests initially in March of the eighth grade year beginning in 1994; requiring all graduates of chartered non-public schools to pass the ninth grade tests beginning in 1999; providing exemptions from the citizenship test for students who are not

U.S. residents, do not intend to remain in the U.S., and attend chartered non-public high schools; and requiring the State Board of Education to develop standards for ethical use of tests ("Background/History,"1998). The April 1994 ruling was set by The State Board of Education and the Governor issued an Executive Order establishing Emergency Rules 3301-13-01 and 3301-13-02 (as amended) and new Rule 3301-13-08 (Trent). The amendments permitted students whose native language is not English to use translation dictionaries and to have additional time for taking any of the tests. The new rule also provided for an oral administration to any student who, by the end of the final semester, meets the curriculum requirements for graduation; has previously taken but not yet passed the test(s); and has either earned a grade point average of 2.5 or higher in high school courses in the same curricular area as the test not yet passed, or whose native language is not English (Trent). The state department continued to pass law in reference to state mandated testing.

> August 1997 the 122nd Ohio General Assembly enacted and the Governor signed into law Amended Senate Bill 55 that phased out the requirement for students to pass Ninth Grade Proficiency Tests; replaced this requirement with a provision for students to pass tests measuring tenth grade proficiency to graduate from high school beginning September 15, 2004; for students entering fourth grade after July 1, 2001, required districts to retain in fourth grade any student who did not pass the fourth grade reading proficiency test unless the teacher and principal agree the student is academically prepared for fifth grade; permitted districts, beginning July 1, 1999, to retain in fourth grade or sixth grade any student who fails three or more proficiency tests; and increased the number of credits needed to graduate (Trent).

There are consequences to the political influences in education, one being increased controversy over decisions made to benefit one group over another, and another is the need for policymakers to pay attention to the arguments of special interests groups and the individual or group espousing the arguments (Rivlin 1973). The Airasian article focus is on standardized testing two roles of monitoring the educational system and certifying individual performance in the system. A variety of different types of tests were used for monitoring, including traditional school based standardized achievement and ability tests, the Scholastic Aptitude Tests, and new state assessment tests that proliferated at this time (Koffler 1984). Individual pupil data was measured and aggregated across pupils, school districts, and often states. This data was used as the primary indicator in monitoring the success or failure of America's educational system. The test results and trends were intended to be monitors of educational policy, not direct motivators of it. In the early stages of testing many of the monitoring tests were administered on a voluntary basis to samples of schools and samples of pupils; it was not important to have test results from every pupil or school in order for the tests to perform their monitoring function. There were no sanctions associated with test performance, so that the motivating "threat" of a sanction for poor performance, which would have made the tests considerably more intrusive, was absent (Airasian). During early testing rarely decisions about individual teachers, pupils, or schools linked to performance on tests were used to monitor educational policy (Airasian). During this time state-mandated certification testing was not used to guide classroom instruction or to monitor educational policy.

Testing evolved through state legislatures or state boards of education for all schools at selected grade or occupation levels. The purpose of the test was to certify the performance of each district or individual. Testing was and still is a statewide instrument administered, scored, and interpreted similarly from district to district according to state guidelines. There are sanctions or rewards associated with test performance. The tests have a built-in requirement and criteria for determining a decision of performance of pass or fail of an individual (Airasian). Standardized tests have become important for decisions involving staff reduction, interschool comparisons, funding allotments, high school graduation, grade-to-grade promotion, program evaluation, and the assessment of educational equity. Society has made the tests themselves important (Airasian).

In Ohio in January 1989 tests and items were developed by curriculum specialists for each test area. The draft specifications were then reviewed by four panels of Ohio educators and other citizens (Trent). These panels included the Testing Steering Committee, a panel of educators representing the diversity of all Ohio's school districts; four content expert panels (one for each area), consisting of teachers and curriculum specialists familiar with curriculum and instruction in grades seven through 12; a bias review panel consisting of persons representing the cultural diversity of Ohio; and a national Technical Advisory Panel, consisting of test and measurement experts both from Ohio and from other parts of the country (Trent). In December 1989 field testing of test questions was completed in approximately 60 Ohio high schools (Trent). The data was used by review panels to approve items for inclusion in the item bank, and by the contractor to select items for the first two forms of the tests, to be administered in November 1990 and March 1991 (Trent). In December 1990 the second field testing of test questions was completed in approximately 60 Ohio high schools. Data was used by the review panels to approve items for inclusion in the item bank, and by the contractor to select items for the third and fourth forms of the tests, to be administered in November 1991 and March 1992 (Trent).

The public seeks some external assurance of the quality of teaching and learning, and it turns to standardized testing for evidence. Test results have brought to light to the public and policy makers differences in the goals and priorities of varied social groups. For example, there is a constant tension between the goals of quality and equality, between the use of tests to improve educational quality and current definitions of equal educational opportunity (Astin et al. 1982; Samuda 1975). Standardized test results are a common index used for comparisons and measurement of quality educational opportunity.

Cynthia Price

Mandated Testing Dilemmas

The controversy of testing is of no surprise as noted in the chart below which was part of Airasian research in 1987. His research points to propositions that were reviewed as commentary and controversy (Airasian 1987) about testing and provides a framework for understanding the present-day context of testing.

Commentary	Controversy
The school is basically a conservative, reactive institution, so one must look to social institutions beyond the school to identify the stresses that produce school change.	Testing takes place in a politicized environment in which the agendas of different interest groups compete for attention.
A change in the goals, functions, or locus of control of the educational process will produce concomitant changes in the tools (e.g., tests, textbooks, curricula, etc.) used to carry out the educational process.	The crucial issues of testing are not technical. Issues of testing today are social, economic, and value-laden, involving the distribution and redistribution of resources and prerogatives
The political benefits of testing often outweigh the educational benefits.	The quantity of educational testing is inversely related to the public's general satisfaction with the educational system.
More and more, understanding and weighing debate over testing cannot be accomplished without consideration of who is espousing the arguments.	Test debate and controversy will be better understood if one bears in mind the distinction between traditional, locally determined test uses and state-mandated test uses.

New tests must be evaluated not only in terms of their technical adequacy but also in terms of the likely social and legal implications of their use.	Two important functions of testing in the policy domain are management and control.

Much of the mandating test narrative is a correlation to the rise and spread of standards that encourage test-based school funding, teacher certification testing, and high school graduation testing. Testing mandates are the root of the current test debate and controversy since these uses of test results involve the distribution or redistribution of educational benefits and resources (Airasian). Standardized testing has become intertwined with social and political issues such as equality, social standards, and control (Airasian). Even though Peter W. Airasian article is dated, the controversies about mandated testing still exist today. Researchers have found valid correlations between the amounts of time spent on testing; tests align to Common Core standards, testing equity, and testing policy align with students' learning objectives.

In March 1994, plaintiffs in the Cleveland desegregation case (Reed vs. Rhodes) challenged the fairness of the test and sought a delay in the use of tests as a graduation requirement (Trent). In a court-ordered settlement, the test requirements were left intact for the Class of 1994. In March 1994, the Office of Civil Rights began an investigation of possible violation of Title VI of the Civil Rights Act (Trent). An Agreement between the Office of Civil Rights and the Department of Education was signed on October 3, 1994, ending OCR'S investigation and leaving the tests intact, without any findings (Trent). In October 1995, the Ohio Association of Independent Schools (OAIS) filed suit in federal district court in Cincinnati on behalf of its 30 member schools challenging the state's requiring member schools to administer the Ninth Grade Tests and students to pass the tests prior to graduating (Trent). In January 1996, the court ruled in favor of the state on all counts. In August 1996, the Sixth Circuit Court of Appeals upheld the decision. Plaintiffs appealed to the U.S. Supreme Court, but the court rejected the appeal without comment (Trent).

The Democratic Lens of Equity

David Tyack examines socioeconomic status (SES) growing rapidly throughout the educational system leaving ideas of inequality in schools. The social class achievement and attainment gaps presented problems for school systems. Minorities often perform lower on achievement tests than their white counterparts and standardized testing has become a controversial issue. Tyack writes in his book Seeking Common Ground that in 1874 students who did not pass promotion tests were referred to as retarded, leftovers, dull, slow, immature, and overgrown (Tyack). Many of the students leftover or behind were impoverished immigrants and blacks and attended urban schools. Urban schools in the 1920's and 1930's created elaborate testing and counseling systems designed to sort students into tracks to help them select courses that would benefit themselves and society.

Changes in educational policy lead the Nixon Administration to propose the Equal Educational Opportunities Act. The bill contained language ensuring equal opportunities for all children (Cross). Ohio set standards in January 1989 test and item specifications were developed by curriculum specialists for each test area (Trent). The draft specifications were then reviewed by four panels of Ohio educators and other citizens. These panels included the Testing Steering Committee, a panel of educators representing the diversity of all Ohio's school districts; four content expert panels (one for each area), consisting of teachers and curriculum specialists familiar with curriculum and instruction in grades seven through 12; a bias review panel consisting of persons representing the cultural diversity of Ohio; and a national Technical Advisory Panel, consisting of test and measurement experts both from Ohio and from other parts of the country (Trent). Standardized testing became a way to "maximize children's life chances" (Gutmann). Maximization in the sense that educational resources would be distributed to the least advantaged children.

Deborah Stone writes that equity is the "who gets what, when, and how." Stone writes the elaborate story of the slices of cake, and explains many different options on how the cake should be sliced. One quote that stuck out is "all sides seek equality; the conflict comes over how the sides envision a fair distribution of whatever is at stake" (Stone). She further explains that equality means the same- size for everyone (Stone). This paradox often leads to distribution problems and often results in inequality or unequal treatment. Stone's research includes the concept of merit in her argument of equity. For example, tests of vocabulary and cultural references are biased and don't measure the knowledge that working-class and minority student gain from their life experience" (Stone). Merit or rewards are given to students whose parents have the money to pay for test-prep courses and students who do not have the funds or opportunity to enhance their studies fall behind. The concept of equity leads to issues of membership, rank, group, and competition.

Standardized Testing

Standardized testing is a tool used to measure student's progress however many Americans says that there is too much emphasis on testing. A 2015 Gallup Survey of the Public Attitudes Toward the Public Schools show that 67 percent of public school parents say that there is too much testing. Included in the survey 14 percent of the parents rated testing as very important. (Walker) The results of the survey reflect the growing number of communities and parents across the nation that have asked lawmakers to consider less testing policies and more time to learn in the classroom.

> "The high stakes obsession of test and punishment has only served to widen the gap between the schools in the wealthiest districts and those in the poorest," says NEA President Lily Eskelsen García. "We must reduce the

emphasis on standardized tests that have corrupted the
quality of the education children receive. The pressure
placed on students and educators is enormous."(Walker)

In some respects standardized tests present an inaccurate picture of student performance and encourage schools to focus on test performance rather than the skills needed to perform well in life. There are a number of tests given in schools but for the state of Ohio there are specific tests that count toward grade transitions and graduation. The tests that count in Ohio are the kindergarten readiness test, tests for English Language Learners (OTELLA), the Ohio Achievement Assessments (OAA) and Ohio Graduation Tests. The Ohio Achievement Assessments are used for student performance in English language arts and math in third, fourth, sixth, and seventh grades. In the fifth grade science and social studies are added to the assessments and students are tested in all four areas in the eighth grade (ODE). The OAA third grade reading test is given in the fall and spring. The Ohio Graduation Tests start in the spring of tenth grade and students have until the spring of twelfth grade to pass all five parts (reading, writing, math, science and social studies). Students must earn a proficient score in each category of the Third grade OAA test in order to pass to the fourth grade (ODE). This is known as the Third Grade Reading Guarantee. Starting in the 2013-14 school year, students who don't score high enough must be held back unless they are still learning English, can demonstrate "reading competency" on other state-approved tests, have a special-education plan that says they can't be held back or meet other requirements (ODE). Students in high school must pass all five parts of the Ohio Graduation Tests in order to earn a high-school diploma.

One question to consider is why are these tests given? The answer is standardized testing is part of the 1994 Elementary and Secondary Education Act (ODE). According to federal legislation all states are required to test students annually. The Elementary and Secondary Education Act was strengthened in 2001 with the passage of the No Child Left Behind Act (ODE) and later replaced with Every Student Success Act (ESSA)

Since 2001 forty-nine states had established content standards and were linking them to testing in key subjects (Cross). Students' test results are directly connected to Adequate Yearly Progress (AYP). Schools, school districts, and states have to show that students across different racial and ethnic groups are progressing toward a goal of proficiency or higher on standardized tests.

The federal Department of Education in 2012 granted Ohio permission to extend the goal of having all students proficient in reading and math by 2014 (ODE). The results of these tests are used in various ways. The results of the OAA are used to measure progress of each student called value added which tell how much progress students make in one academic year. Schools that perform poorly on state test are subject to consequences. Public schools with low test scores have to change how they operate. Schools in this situation could replace staff, use new curriculum, and may become eligible for extra support for turnaround efforts (ODE).

Testing Standards

The State of Ohio changed the state curriculum to Common Core Standards. This is a national set of expectations that all students are to meet at each grade level. The new standards brought a new test called Partnership for Assessment of Readiness for College and Careers (PARCC). This test was put in place for one year (2014) until policy makers, teachers, students, and parents became unsatisfied. This past year (2015) Ohio picked American Institutes for Research (AIR) testing to replace PARCC testing and this decision has created a controversy. The state previously had a multi-state partnership with both testing centers. AIR provided previous state tests including the Ohio Achievement Assessments and the Ohio Graduation Tests. The decision to replace PARCC was backed by legislation and gives Ohio opportunities to design their own test with Ohio educators in conjunction with AIR experts.

Cynthia Price

The Ohio Department of Education presented a new policy for testing English Language Arts in Ohio. The new assessment for the 2015-2016 school year in English language arts is:

> Per the new law, Ohio will cease the use of PARCC tests in English language arts. Instead, the Ohio Department of Education will use our existing contract with the American Institutes for Research (AIR) – which currently provides online science and social studies assessments – to provide Ohio's English language arts tests. The new tests will use the same testing platform and other services that AIR already provides to Ohio. These will be Ohio's tests and will align to Ohio's standards.

The tests will be online and paper versions of the tests will be available for schools who are not "technology-ready" (ODE). The test will be given two times a year at the beginning of the year and later in the spring so that student's progress is monitored. Policy makers put some safeguards in place to protect the students from excessive testing. The test will be shorter than tests given last school year, administered once per year in a single testing window, and given during the second half of the school year. High schools may give end-of-course tests in the first semester, and provide results no later than June 30 of each school year. Third grade reading results will return no later than June 15 (ODE). Revisions of the policy are recommended accommodations for Limited Language Learner and Special Education students. These accommodations would include but not limited to IEP specifications, OTELLA test results for Limited Language Learners (LLL) and 504 accommodations. These accommodations would also include oral test administration, the use of a dictionary for translation purposes, and extended time accommodations.

Students Learning Objectives Study

Standardized tests preparation extends to the classroom teachers use student learning objectives to track student's progress throughout the year. These objectives are a segment of teacher professional development. Columbus City Schools teacher evaluation system uses Student Learning Objectives (SLO's) to measure student growth. This measurement is accomplished by using pre and post tests. Teachers collect samples from two classes and measure student's growth through testing and classroom assignments. My SLO for the 2013-2014 school year involved the district Scholastic Reading Inventory (SRI) test. I proposed that students would improve their (SRI) score by at least 15 points within six months of the 2013-2014 school year. Students would take the test at the beginning of the year 9/2013 and repeat the test before 04/2014.

SLO Research and Results

There were 14 students in the class (1) IEP, and (13) regular education students. Nine students were proficient readers, four were basic readers, and one was below basic in reading. The interval of instruction was 9/2013 - 04/2014. The class meant 80 minutes every day. The class was sectioned into four (20 minutes) time periods (Reading Showcase, Students Literature Teams, Focus Lesson, and Self Selected Reading or Learning Centers). The objective, lesson, assignment, and exit ticket were posted on the board daily. The class used folders to organize their assignments and assessments.

Students engaged in lessons which cited textual evidence that supported inferences and analysis of stories. Students read and comprehend literature at the nine grade level by using a Prentice Hall Literature text appropriate to the grade level. The reinforcement assignments contained reading inventory of selected topics, and guided questions to selected passages. The last assessment was a repeated SRI test. Students demonstrated learning with completion and processing stories through critical thinking questions, cooperative and collaborative learning, graphic charts, and visual learning. Students practiced reading techniques such as before, during and after reading analysis. Students read passages from the Prentice Hall Literature English 9 text.

The pre-assessment for the SLO was the SRI test and the post-assessment was a SRI test. The cooperative learning assignments in between the pre/ post tests built student's fluency, comprehension and analysis. The growth target for students was to increase their reading level score by 15 points. Students increased literacy and comprehension skills by processing texts through means of chunking, context clues, inferences, stated, and implied means of assessments.

I proposed that half the students increased their score by 15 points to move from below basic to basic. However one student was below grade level and below basic, five students were basic and eight students were on grade level and proficient. Students read and comprehend informational text appropriate for the 9th grade. Students determined a central idea in a text, and analyzed how its development was shaped through details. Students used textual evidence to support analysis of what the text says explicitly as well as inferences drawn from the text. Based on the growth patterns each student would increase lexile score by 15 points in order to move grade levels, or achieve basic and proficient grades. The results are as follows: 5 students most effective, 4 above average, 3 average, 1 approaching average, and 1 least effective. 93% exceeding / meeting target, 7% below target. The chart below is a record of the pre and post scores and growth measured.

Student Baseline Score   Growth Final Score Exceed/Meets Target

Student	Baseline Score	Growth	Final Score	Exceed/Meets Target
D	861	208	1069	yes
Ma	809	69	878	yes
Ki	936	-30	906	no

Tj	1112	28	1140	yes
Tq	1063	33	1096	yes
So	1145	3 (baseline score		
proficient)	1148	yes		
C	951	21	972	yes
H	1178	-50 (baseline score proficient)	1128	yes
St	280	120	400	yes
Ka	825	14 (final score falls within growth percentage)		
	839	yes		
Al	1037	4 (baseline score proficient)	1041	yes
An	1037	(baseline score proficient)	1037	yes
M	1260	77	1337	yes
Cw	744	46	790	yes

Student learning objectives are measurable, long-term academic growth targets that a teacher sets at the beginning of the year for all students. The teacher or school creates and administers student learning objective tests to measure each student's progress on each growth target. Tests are given twice a year; once at the beginning of the year and again at the end of the year (Testing Report). In addition to student learning objective tests largely contributing to the time students spend taking tests, the department has heard many criticisms from teachers and administrators that student learning objectives are too time-consuming and create equity issues between categories of teachers. Because teachers create and grade their own student learning objective tests, some claim there is an opportunity to manipulate student performance (Testing Report).

School districts have sought flexibility from state testing requirements to implement new, innovative education programs. Until recent legislative action, state and federal law did not allow the department to offer this flexibility. In June 2014, the General Assembly passed a law that created an innovative school waiver pilot program (Testing Report). The pilot gives up to 10 school districts and Science, Technology, Engineering, and Math (STEM) schools the chance to apply for a temporary exemption from state testing and other requirements so they can try alternative methods of assessing their students' learning (Testing Report).

Mandated Testing Dilemmas

The Ohio Department of Education is working with the American Institutes of Research to provide testing services in Ohio. The partnership will build new math and English language arts tests for the spring of 2016. The process being used this year will give Ohio educators maximum control to ensure that the questions align with the learning stands while also meeting aggressive deadlines for producing the test. The following steps for testing were set by ODE.

1. Ohio has built a five step pathway to Standardized Testing. The first step is ODE identifies which learning standards will be tested in each grade and subject.

2. Second, the blueprints are published for each grade and subject. The blueprints list the standards to be tested and the percentage of test questions associated with the standard. Test questions from AIR that have been field tested are provided to ODE. The questions were taken by sample groups of students in other states. Questions were judged to be reliable and become candidates for use in an actual test.

3. The third step is ODE reviews the questions to ensure that each is aligned to standards that Ohio has chosen to test.

4. The fourth step is a committee of Ohio teachers and other stakeholders review sets of questions and select those that can appear on a test.

5. The fifth step is ODE and AIR build online and paper tests by selecting from the list of questions approved by the review committee.

Standardized testing is a major component of the educational system. State and federal policy makers set guidelines and reward funding based on the success of school systems. Schools are dated with formal, informal, standardized (performance standards), and short cycle assessments. Most states have a state test that must be passed before a diploma is granted. Standards based assessments have contributed to inequalities in schools. Some teachers teach to the test and as a result limit opportunities for diversity and equity in classrooms. The tests do not take into account cultural and learning disabilities differences. Ohio will spend millions of dollars to prevent test biases. The Ohio Department of Education is committed to collaborate with AIR, districts and schools to seek U.S. Department of Education approval for using alternative, state-approved assessment systems. Testing recommended accommodations for Limited Language Learner and Special Education students are still in the early stages of negotiations. Testing regulations should include special accommodations for IEP, Limited Language Learners (LLL) and 504 students. These accommodations should include oral test administration, the use of a dictionary for translation purposes, and extended time accommodations.

CHAPTER 10

PROFESSIONAL PLAN

I used the book <u>Connecting Teacher Leadership and School Improvement</u>, by Joseph Murphy to guide me through the process of Teacher Leadership. I felt the book offered key ideas to the necessary stages of teacher leadership and school reform. The second chapter "Forces Supporting Teacher Leadership", is meaningful because currently there is a Teacher Leadership Certification offered in my district. The second cohort is starting Fall of 2017. This is an opportunity that the district has extended to teachers to create new paths of leadership which was mentioned in the book. The book states "there is an emerging conception of leadership and successful organization depending on multiple sources of leadership." (Murphy p. 29) The following steps of action will enhance my professional plan.

I created a notebook for evidence of professional development. I used the research of the 150 50 Project and presented teacher professional development around the district. The PP 150 50 Project includes presenting research about how to monitor students to achieve success. The plan included an qualitative action research case study (QUAL-quan) method with a purposive sample size of 9th grade students. The study revealed literacy skills and how literacy skills evolved over the year to increase Scholastic Reading Inventory (SRI) score. Students showed gains in student achievement and literacy skills. The study included English Second Language students, Special Education students and regular education students. The process included a team of Ninth grade teachers, administrators, school curriculum coaches, community partners, City Year Corp members in the classroom, and applied I, II, III tiered interventions.

Teachers were inspired to go back to their schools and ask their leadership to adopt this Project. The project includes a plan for building leadership to allow the teachers to meet in teams during the school day so the data collection and meetings can take place. The school would need Community Partners from City Year and Communities in Schools.

The PD should be scheduled for two days. The plan involves the cooperation of the administration. The projetct needs to have buy-in from the district and pilot schools. The plan starts with freshmen students and then matriculates to the sophomores the following year, therefore training will begin with freshmen teachers. Teacher Leaders would be trained to collect data, develop agendas for meetings, report out at staff meetings, assist teachers with I and II tiered inventions, and set up meetings with students and parents. The following guidelines are suggested.

> Student Learning Objectives: A student learning objective is a measurable, long-term academic growth target that a teacher sets at the beginning of the year for all students or for subgroups of students. Student learning objectives demonstrate a teacher's impact on student learning (ODE).

> Academics Value Added: Analytical approach to see how students are progressing and which teaching methods were having the greatest impact (ODE).

> Academics: Monitoring students through the Every Student Succeeds Act (ESSA), a long-awaited overhaul of federal education law. Passed with bipartisan support, ESSA represents a shift from broad federal oversight of

primary and secondary education to greater flexibility and decision making at the state and local levels. The law replaces the No Child Left Behind Act (following ODE state and district curriculum).

Ohio is committed to involving educators, parents and other stakeholders as we explore new ways to ensure that all our students receive the education they need for bright futures (ODE). ESSA requires that states develop plans that address standards, assessments, school and district accountability, and special help for struggling schools (ODE). One way to achieve this goal is to have City Year in the classroom and Community In Schools helping with the monitoring system.

Behavior: Response to Intervention (RTI) is a multi-tier approach to the early identification and support of students with learning and behavior needs. Multi-tiered System of Supports (MTSS) as an integrated, multi-tiered system of instruction, assessment, and intervention designed to meet the achievement and behavioral health needs of ALL learners. In short, an MTSS framework is designed to ensure that each and every student that walks into a classroom will have his or her individual needs met through high-quality instruction (MDE).

Attendance: Students with regular school attendance are more successful academically and have more opportunities for important communications with their teachers. They also feel a stronger sense of connection with both their peers and the school community. Attendance is a preventative approach to excessive absences and truancy. Districts will amend or adopt policies that outline their interventions and plans for students who miss too much school. According to Ohio law schools cannot suspend or expel students for missing too much school. The 150 50 Project proposes:

- o Notification of student absence to the parent or guardian
- o Development and implementation of an absence intervention plan, which may include supportive services for students and families
- o Counseling
- o Parent education and parenting programs
- o Mediation
- o Intervention programs available through juvenile authorities

This model will require a change in district policy so that the plan can serve and benefit all stakeholders. The district would put in place board policy that allow schools to implement the 150 50 Project: district and teacher's professional development. The district would have to provide resources (books, teacher leaders monitoring system, the cost of professional development, and stakeholder's incentives / stipends, student's rewards, allocated site based budget). Support teachers with creating student learning objectives which are measurable, long-term academic growth targets that teachers set at the beginning of the year for all students or for subgroups of students. Student learning objectives demonstrate a teacher's impact on student learning.

The 150 50 Project connects to district personnel to encourage the district to allow Teacher Leaders to be trained to collect data, develop agendas for meetings, report out at staff meetings, assist teachers with I and II tiered inventions, and set up meetings with students and parents. The book Connecting Teacher Leadership and School Improvement supports new reforms and power distribution,

> "a perspective that assumes the schools can be improved by distributing political power among the various groups who have legitimate interests in the nature and quality of educational services. Reforms that seek to reallocate power and authority among various stakeholders are

based on the belief that when power is in the right hands, schools will improve." (41)

The book provides information about "role-based and community-based strategies" in chapter five "Pathways to Teacher Leadership" to develop the teacher leadership position. The role -based strategies include teacher career and broadening administrative and structures and roles. The community-based strategies are shared leadership and communities of practice.

The 150 50 Project is delivered in three parts which are Behavior Modifications in the classroom, Attendance Plan (HB 410), and Monitoring Academics. I have worked on an ELA I Content Advisory Committee (January 2017 and August 2017 with Ohio Department of Education to develop lesson plans and coach teachers to successful monitoring of academics with a focus on literacy. I used the feedback forms from the 150 50 Project to increase educational opportunities in the school. Supporting teachers with creating measurable student learning objectives which contain long-term academic growth targets that teachers used in their classrooms. I have recommended and presented articles, books and videos to the teachers and administration. The following materials were used in the 150 50 Project presentation.

- Connecting Teacher Leadership and School Improvement
- "White Teachers in Urban Classrooms: Embracing Non-White Students' Cultural Capital For Better Teaching and Learning" By Barry M. Goldenberg
- Teaching- Explore and Challenge Equity

Teachers gained understanding of diversity, equity, and inclusion in the classroom. All three components affect a student's achievement. Teachers gained insight on diversity and equity programs that districts and teachers used to support ELL, ELA and Special education students.

These topics impose barriers for social change in schools. The question of how educational goods should be equitably distributed remains a controversial topic. Bourdieu's research depends on the cultural capital networks available and used by schools. In order to increase cultural and social capitals in schools, students should learn standards, norms, values, beliefs and these norms are helpful agents and coping strategies in society.

Cultural capital is effectively transmitted within schools and the family and depends on the quantity and quality accumulation. The more cultural capital is prevented from being transferred the circle of inequalities continues in schools.

CHAPTER 11

TEACHER LEADERSHIP ENDORSEMENT

The TLE process includes competencies of Reflective Practice and Continuing Learning. I included diversity and equity in every phase of my plan. These units have led me to Policy Advocacy. The TLE process has given me encouragement, structure and avenues to put my school reform in place.

My personal vision is, I am passionate about education. I have been both a teacher and Leadership Intern (Assistant Principal) in Columbus City Schools. I have been taking courses for several years at The Ohio State University in the Department of Educational Studies. These courses have improved my teaching, learning and leadership experiences. I started this process with a plan to build a reform model that addressed students' behaviors (Zoom video and powerpoint), academics (Student Learning Objectives sample lessons), and attendance (House Bill 410 power point). I chose to focus on the Behaviors Modifications powerpoint which is one segment of the 150 50 Reform Model. The power point Behavior Modifications reflects my mission statement that addresses teacher to student relationships. The purpose of the powerpoint is to explain Behaviors Modifications as it relates to time on task and instructional time in the classroom. This power point has helped teachers examine how student's behaviors are addressed in the classroom.

The 150 50 Project is needed in my district so that all high school students have equal opportunities. There are 21 high schools total in the district, three of the schools are bridge schools (career, technology, and performing arts). Students that attend these schools are sent back to their home school to graduate. The performance index of 18 high schools range from D to F, value added scores range from A- D, and graduation rates range from A-F. As shown the district high school divisions are in dire need of reform. I have chosen to introduce the 150 50 Project to Mifflin High School (my school of eight years) because we were a Diplomas Now school for five years and Mifflin has the background developed for the 150 50 Reform.

The power point (Behavior Modifications) was first shown to five selected teachers. The five teachers were asked to view the powerpoint and provide feedback. I reviewed their comments and made changes to sentence structure and added articles to strengthen my points on building social relationships with students. My principal asked me early in September to present the powerpoint at the professional development on September 22, 2017. I presented the revised power point to the Mifflin High School teachers and administration. I asked them to provide feedback on my presentation. Since the face-to-face presentation I have revised the Behavior Modifications powerpoint (for the second time). My next steps are to present the HB 410 power point, Educational Opportunities in Cooperative Learning: A Guide for Interaction and Achievement Using the 150 50 Project and Communities In Schools podcast.

The (Behavior Modifications) powerpoint with a restorative practice activity. During the powerpoint I asked teachers to read the social relationship article and then teachers discussed the article in small groups and then together as a whole group. Teachers were asked to discuss corrective behavior practices used in their classroom. Teachers embraced the ideas of behavior modifications of: Response to Intervention (RTI) a multi-tier approach to the early identification and support of students with learning and behavior needs. Multi-tiered System of Supports (MTSS) is an integrated, multi-tiered system of instruction, assessment, and intervention designed to meet the achievement and behavioral health needs of ALL learners. In short, an MTSS framework is designed to ensure that students that walk into a classroom will have his or her individual needs met through high-quality instruction.

My leadership and designs are displayed in the (150 50 Project) the behavior modifications plan is phase one of the reform. Phase two includes research about how to monitor students to achieve success. The research is a qualitative action research case study (QUAL-quan) method with purposive sample size of 9th grade students. The study reveals literacy skills and how literacy skills evolved over the year to increase Scholastic Reading Inventory (SRI) score. Students showed gains in student achievement and literacy skills. There were two groups one was English Second Language students; Special Education students and the other class was regular education students. The process includes a team of Ninth grade teachers, administrators, school curriculum coaches, community in schools, City Year Corp, and applied I, II, III tiered interventions.

PART II
RESEARCH OF DIVERSITY EQUITY AND INCLUSION
(DEI)

"FACTORS OF RACE CONSCIOUSNESS"

The period of Black unrest in the 1960's was a time in U.S. history very influential of the direction which the social sciences chose. During this time the social sciences acquired an interest in the study of Black attitudes.

The goal of this research is to pursue a specific area of Black attitudes, race consciousness among Black undergraduates at majority White institutions. The definition to be used is James Pitts', "it is normative behavior which develops in a racially stratified environment. Actions this may include is to see your race as an entity, and to feel obligation toward one's groups" Pitts, 1974, p. 677).

Questions which this research will probe are varied. The first is whether race consciousness exists despite the recent absences of Black insurgency. The second, is the paradigm of race consciousness one norm or several. The last is, how do variables such as urban, region, participation in Black activities, and variables dealing with perception of society affect race consciousness.

The first area of exploration is whether there is race consciousness without recent uprising. This point is determined by the state of race consciousness today, and to see what forms it takes outside the mass organizing of peaceful protest or rioting.

The second area is introduced as a point which may clarify research in this area. This area is to examine the possibility that race consciousness is not one concept, but several.

Finally, the research will seek to find the effect of variables such as urban, region, and social class (of the student), the extent of participation by the student in Black social activities, and Black Studies, and perception variables such as whether the students s internally, or externally directed, and the amount of discrimination the student perceives against themselves.

Perspectives

There are three works which are essential for study in the area of race consciousness among Black College Students: Black Consciousness, Identity, and Achievement by Patricia Gurin, and Edgar Epps, "The Nature and Context of Black Nationalism of Northwestern in 1971" by Freddye Hill, and "The Politicalization of Black Students" by James P. Pitts.

In Black Consciousness, Identity, and Achievement, Black students of Black colleges were studied in regards to student activism, civil rights activism, and ideological support of race consciousness. They found that from 1964 to 1970 there had been a change in perception among students, and civil rights activists.

In 1964 activists were efficacious and held the opinion that their action would make a difference, but in 1970 it was not efficacy which predicted activism but Black Nationalism and system blame (Gurin, Epps, 1975[,] pp.275-279). Also, it was found that on campuses known for activism that the activists were the most popular, as well as brightest students; whereas on non-activist campuses activist were found to be marginal students who did not fit in as well (Gurin, Epps, 1975, pp. 310-315).

In Hill's work there is a shift in focus from what variables affect race consciousness to how many norm race consciousness contains. Hill obtains this answer by employing a technique known as Guttman Scaling. With this technique Hill discovers that there are two kinds of race consciousness: (1) Separatist, which supported such themes as a Black Nation, separation of Black from Whites, and (2) and Afro Scale which supported unification of Black with oppressed people (Hill, 1975, pp. 324-328).

The last of the essential works in this area is "The Politicalization of Black Students". In this work Pitts tells of the gradual development of the Black student group at Northwestern (For Members Only, or F.M.O.), when a large influx of newly admitted Blacks enrolled.

First F.M.O. is described as a social group, later is slowly developed into a racially conscious group with the purpose of organizing function of the group (Pitts, 1975, pp. 277-316).

Method

The perspectives above provide a variety of research methods used to explore race consciousness from the use of Guttman Scaling in Hill's case to Participant Observation used by Pitts. In this research the method used will be a mixture between categorization of race consciousness presented by Hill, and the survey research approach offered by Gurin and Epps.

Ten questions were used to determine race consciousness (previously used by Epps). These ten questions were factor analyzed, and from them three indices were constructed representing three dependent variables. The first of these indices were called "Black Problems Need Black Solutions". To score high on this index the student had to support the concept of a National Black Party, not accept interracial dating and marriage as the status quo, support the idea that majority Black schools should have majority Black teachers, and disagree that Black students have the same problems as Whites.

The second index was entitled "Mobilization for Future Progress". High scores on this index believed that the church had helped Blacks, that there was unity and sharing among Blacks at their university, and that the future looked promising for young Blacks.

The third index was "Blacks aren't Divided"/ To score high one had to disagree with Black men and women not getting along, middle class Blacks are more similar to middle class Whites, and participation in organized athletics is usually harmful to Black college students.

With the above three dependent variables it is planned to use three multiple regressions. The independent variables included: sex, rural, urban (of the student), region (the student if from), social class, internally/ externally directed, university G.P.A., participation in Black social activities, perceived frequency of discrimination, whether the student has in the past enrolled in a Black Studies course, and university major.

Data

The data which will be used to test the three aforementioned equations will come from a cross sectional study of 695 Black undergraduates. The universities included in this study were: University of Michigan, University of North Carolina Chapel Hill, University of New York Stony Brook, Memphis State University, University of California Los Angeles, and Arizona State. The data for this study was collected in the spring thru summer of 1981.

Results

In the first equation with the dependent variable index of Black Problems need Black Solutions", and the independent variables mentioned before, a

F stat was obtained of 6.52 (prob value of near .000). Of all the independent variables mentioned sex, and perception of amount of discrimination are approaching significance with prob values of .14, and .055 respectively.

Individual variables which are significant are: enrollment in Black Studies (prob value .007), participation in Black social activities (prob value .03), and the external degree of the subject (prob value .0001).

In the second equation with the dependent variable of "Mobilization for Future Progress", and the same independent variables as in equation one, there was a F stat of 2.19 (prob value .02). Individually the variables which seemed to play the largest part in the significance of the model were the rural/urban variables with the more urban scoring the highest (prob value .03), and the participation in Black activities also playing a large part (prob value .005). The externally directed subject variable approached significance (prob value .11), as did the enrollment in Black Studies (prob value.29).

The final equation "Blacks aren't Divided" (with the same independent variables as the others) was not significant with a F stat of 1.06 (prob value .40). In this equation there was not one variable which was significant, but the ones which approached significance were: perception of discrimination, having enrolled before in a Black Studies course, and participation in Black activities with respective prob values of .07, .2, .12.

From the three equations above it seems that perception of the amount of discrimination, enrollment in Black Studies, participation in Black social activities, and the externality of the student are the most influential variables through all three equations. These four variables mentioned above consistently showed the lowest prob values.

Importance

It is clear that although this proposal speaks of the experience of Blacks; concepts in this research can be applied to most oppressed groups. In other words, most groups when singled out for discrimination form similar allegiances, and see their group as separate. These reactions can lead to the direct challenging and eventual toppling of such discriminatory practices.

Another aspect of importance can be seen as an educational issue. This issue is Black Culture, which in many cases was enhanced and developed by the formation of racial consciousness. This can be seen merely by looking at the preliminary results; the strongest significance in all three models goes to variables dealing with participation in Black Studies, and Black social events. Therefore, this research is important for scientific as well as educational purposes.

TRANSFORMING THE IMAGE OF THE AFRICAN AMERICAN MAN

Kehinde Wiley is an African American painter who has played a tremendous role in reviving the image of the black man. Born in 1977, Wiley has at first hand experienced the consequences that the stereotypical perceptions that Americans have created of the black man have caused. The African American man has had a limited and diminished role in American society, bound to the historical representations of them from slavery days. Through his recreations of sixteenth, seventeenth, eighteenth, and nineteenth century western art, Kehinde Wiley has shed light on a different side of the African American man, a side as diverse and powerful as himself.

Kehinde Wiley first set out not only to disfigure the narrow view that America has of the black man, but also to address the absence of the black man as a subject in the art world. Raised by his mother in Los Angeles and never knowing his father as a child, Wiley visited art museums and classes with his mother frequently. (Knafo 5) Here he developed a love for western portraiture. However, despite his admiration for the works Wiley was struck by how foreign they were to him. He recalls this incident saying, "Since I felt somewhat removed from the imagery, personally and culturally, I had a scientific approach and aesthetic fascination with the paintings" (Knafo 5).

This fascination grew into a determination to include his own personal and cultural identity into the great masterpieces of the western world. Thus his journey began to place black and brown men in the previous positions of powerful Europeans. Instead of seeing Audries Stilte in his feathered hat and blue and pink silk attire as John Cornelisz Verspronck painted him in 1640, we see a young black man in a white t-shirt, blue jeans, and timberland boots in Wiley's interpretation. Likewise, in place of St. John the Baptist with his tattered robe and crucifix as Spanish painter El Greco shows him in 1600, we see another young black man in a polo shirt, jean shorts, and Air Jordan tennis shoes in Wiley's version. Wiley attests to this process, stating, "I create something akin to the diorama in that the figure is situated in a contrived, constructed space, but I'm also borrowing from images from, say, the ascension Christ and placing Black bodies there" (Knafo 8) .

Kehinde Wiley's paintings also address the limited representations of African American men as it pertains to the diversity of personality, sexuality, and masculinity. Wiley, who is an openly gay man, certainly does not fit into the stereotypically ultra-masculine, hypersexual, and homophobic role that not only larger America but also black America has created of the black man. From music to film to athletics to television the only consistent image of the African American man is that of one who is heterosexual, harsh, and physical, with hip-hop characteristics. Kehinde Wiley's aim was not to eliminate this possibility of an African American man, but to provide more possibilities to the American public as well as illustrate the unconventional beauty of these men. In order to do this, Wiley specifically targeted the feminine aspects of historical European art that were previously viewed as acceptable attributes for men to possess. Wiley's works reflect both the soft, feminine colors, and the feminine mannerisms of the subjects of the time. An article from the Newington-Cropsey Cultural Studies Center comments on Wiley's style saying, "By using young men, posed in attitudes more familiar in icons of feminine virtue, Wiley also raises questions about gender-image" (Newington 1). As is evident in his Portrait of Andries Stilte II and his St. John the Baptist II, Wiley integrates the conventional hip-hop clothing of today's young black men with the feminine traits and colors worn by Europeans. By incorporating this historical edge with the contemporary hip-hop street style of his modern subjects he suggests that both aspects can co-exist, further promoting the diversity of black men like himself.

Perhaps the most important message of Kehinde Wiley's works is the significance of power, wealth, and prestige as it relates to the black man. In America where none of these traits necessarily have been associated with black men, Wiley's paintings suggest a shift in attitude in which African American men represent just as much authority and status as their European counterparts. Wiley communicates this through a combination of colors, body positioning, and size. In any of his pieces the viewer will see that the richest of colors are used with exquisite emphasis on both the subject and the backdrop. Taking from the periods he imitates, Wiley incorporates some type of baroque or rococo pattern in the background of all of his paintings adding extensively to the richness of the portrait. Similarly, the attire of the young black men in his paintings is developed with equal prominence to imitate the importance of the apparel in the original works. The body positioning of the subjects also adds to the attributes of confidence and power. In his Portrait of Audries Stilte II the young black subject stands with poise throwing his head up haughtily with his hand at his waist, just as his St. John the Baptist II depicts the man standing straight and gazing directly at the viewer as if demanding respect. In addition to this, Wiley uses the size and scale of his paintings to also instill power and respect. He purposely makes all of his works larger than life with most spanning from floor to ceiling. In an interview Wiley describes his logic for this stating, "Many people see the size of these paintings and say it's cheap, tacky, even rude, and I guess that's the point. By making them this large it's as if they're saying we refuse to go away quietly" (Wiley). This strategy forces the message to the viewer that African American men are just as commanding as the white men his paintings imitate as well as the white men in today's society, and therefore are just as deserving of a place in documented history.

Cynthia Price

Kehinde Wiley has devoted his career to purging the narrow stereotypical image of the African American man and revealing the power, diversity, and confidence of African American men, like himself, that exist in today's world. As an artist he has worked to include the many attributes of African American men that are present in reality. He has utilized the historical European works as an instrument to implement change, mixing the old with the new and the rational with the irrational to arrive at a concept of the black man that is far from what would meet the superficial eye of society.

TEACHER REFLECTION

I came from a Rural to Urban setting when I arrived in Columbus. I did not pay immediate attention to the school system but soon I developed an interest in the largest school system Columbus Public Schools. I read about the schools in the Columbus Dispatch and Call Post newspapers. I soon recognized that students in Columbus had a very different education when compared to where I grew up (rural setting). I researched these differences when I became a writer for the Black newspaper on campus called Dimensions.

My research began with the desegregation of Columbus schools. Over the years I was fortunate to have conversations with some of the people in Columbus City Schools. Even though Education was not my first degree, I still found an attraction to urban schools. I volunteered in the schools during the 80's and decided to sub in the 90's. I tested the waters of subbing and decided to get my license in 1992. I enrolled in the LEAD program at Ohio Dominican University and completed the program in 1995.

I guess I could be called a continuing education guru. I continued my educational pursuit and I read and collected notes about segregation and desegregation.I discovered that my interests and beliefs were confirmed. There is no *Getting Around Brown!*

This was at the beginning of my teaching career. I started collecting data on my teaching style and teaching daily operations. I taught a Strategic

Cynthia Price

Reading course which aligned students with reading strategies to increase their lexile score, fluency, and comprehension. Most students attended regularly but some students were tardy and absent. This information was not a surprise because absenteeism is a problem in high school. Sometimes students stop coming to school for many reasons.

Students disappeared and reappeared on my roster in the second semester. I developed a re-entry plan for students and was happy to see the students return and was happy to know that school was where they felt safe. One student started to engage in the class by asking questions, doing extra work and tried to get caught up. He was eager to begin the second semester course Literature English 9. He completed most of his assignments and maintained a 75% average. He volunteered to read aloud, worked in groups, and completed independent work.

This time in class he was more vocal about his life situation. He was tardy to school and class but at least he would make it to English. He began to talk about his relationships in school and at home. He disagreed with teachers and his parents about rules that he had to follow. One example was that he wanted to drive to school and his parents would not let him. He had a complete disregard for the fact that he was not old enough to drive. He disputed any rationale that was presented to him. He insisted that he still wanted and needed transportation.

The student would come to class and start an argument in the class. Sometimes it would be about his situations in life. Conversations would turn negatively on other students in the classroom. One day after class I noticed the student was in the attendance office on the phone. I walked in the office to ask him if he was talking to his parents. He said that he was talking with his mother. I asked to speak to her and he replied only if you say good things about me.

I introduced myself and talked positively about the student. I expressed to the mother that the student could have a B in the class if he would apply himself a little more. I explained to her the areas of improvement and she agreed to help her son in those areas. I gave the phone back to the student and started to walk out of the office. Later that day the student caught up with me and thanked me for saying good things about him to his mother. I thought this was a good time to mention to him that we still needed to work on skills which would help him with his grades. He agreed and we walked back to my classroom to develop a plan.

The student realized that relationships at school are important. He needed that opportunity of his mother's attention along with his teacher's guidance to help him visualize that change comes from within. The student connected with teachers and began working in his community. He developed a new awareness about his behaviors and he started coming to school regularly.

There are many missing pieces to this story, some of which a teacher will never know but the point is there are many students in the system who have problems in life which makes them at risk in school. Teachers take students as they come regardless of their situations in school and life. Sometimes students enter the ninth grade with a second grade reading level. The question is, how does this happen? State legislation does not stop to ask how or why these situations occur. Legislators continue to change the standards offering little support that addresses the real problems in schools. The main question is how does a researcher use the concept of cultural capital to make improvements in the educational system?

By broadening the types of cultural capital that are valued in the classroom, I believe that teachers can act as agents of transformation rather than reproduction of inequality. Through a teacher's curriculum, pedagogy and assessment, teachers can either:silence students by denying their voice, that is, by refusing to allow them to speak from their own histories, experiences, and social positions, or [they] can enable them to speak by being attentive to how different voices can be constituted within specific pedagogical relations so as to engage their histories and experiences in both an affirmative and critical way.] (Giroux 1990, 91)

Cynthia Price

[Delpit (1997) would argue that teachers can make a difference for these students by using visible pedagogic models: taking nothing for granted and making explicit the rules of that culture through examples, illustrations and narratives that facilitate the acquisition of school knowledge.

Teachers can act as change agents for creating types of cultural capital in the classroom. Teachers can use curriculum, pedagogy and assessment to help students build their cultural capital. Teachers can also use "specific pedagogical relations to engage students' histories and experiences in both an affirmative and critical way." (Giroux 1990, 91) "Delpit (1997) would argue that teachers can make a difference for these students by using visible pedagogic models: taking nothing for granted and making explicit the rules of that culture through examples, illustrations and narratives that facilitate the acquisition of school knowledge."

A PRISON NARRATIVE

There were five people in our group visiting a Men's Prison Facility, four women and a man. We arrived at approximately 9:30 a.m. and entered the reception area of the prison, where we were told by the receptionist and a woman guard, wearing a gun, to sign in. After we had all signed in, the string of restrictions began; we were told to take everything out of our pockets except an I.D., and that we would not be allowed to take paper and pencil inside the prison (these items were placed in lockers provided by the prison.

The above is an account of the atmosphere which was presented to us as students by the Men's Facility Staff. What particularly struck me about the above was that we could not even take a piece of paper and pencil into the prison, and I am a veteran of visiting prisons and have not encountered a rule such as this at other prison facility Ohio. These were not the only instances where we were restricted. We were detained for thirty minutes trying to clear a woman in our group for entrance. Her name for some reason was not on the list, we viewed it as continuous programs, and were not afforded the opportunity to view the cell block nor talk to inmates.

In essence in our tour we were hand guided through the facility and shown what the administration wanted us to see: the new prison. This is most appropriately shown by the fact that we spent only about an hour in the prison itself all with one administrator, never talking to any inmates. For this reason, most of this paper will focus on staff perception of the program.

Programs

In our conversation with our guide we found that there were two programs, the education program, and the work program. The education program we found was at two levels: the G.E.D. and the associates degree. We found that the educational program was standardized throughout most penal systems so that if an inmate were transferred he did not lose any time in his education because of the transfer. Also, we found out that both the G.E.D. and one associate degree were free, but a B.A or a B.S. were not offered at this prison. If it were, it was explained to us that the inmate would have to pay for it.

The other program which was mentioned was a work plan where people applied for jobs like: clerk, maintenance, or cook (there were no prison industries at this prison). Work was said to be totally voluntary, and that sometimes it was possible to gain skills in such areas as carpentry, plumbing, and maintenance in general, but no certificates were given.

Staff Perception of the Program

The philosophy of our guide on these programs can basically be boiled down to one statement which the guide mentioned several times during our visit: "If a person wants to change, it is hard, and if they don't want to change, it is impossible." After the above he argued that the staff did not feel giving an inmate an education made them a better person, but that it gave them the tools to work with should they choose to go straight. The guide did say that programs are in danger because of the money crunch, but he never stated any new programs which he felt might be helpful if there were money to implement them.

What was stated above fairly represents our guide's position on the programs inside the prison. The guide represented his role as a treatment agent in a passive light. It is worth mentioning that he views inmates as people who need to change. This is a very psychological notion which he proposes for treatment and seems to be an extension of a medical model of prison therapy. This approach has in the past been the main presenter of the attitude of "I know you're poor, unemployed, and possess no skills, but why is it that you are crazy?"

A second area which his perceptions lead me to believe is that no new programs could be used. True, he mentioned that the educational program might be cut back, but he did not once talk about additional programs which might be useful. Also surprising was that only one program was fully developed (the educational program), and the other one (the job program) which would always be there was untouched as a program. This is to say the main emphasis behind the work program was mainly just to keep the prison running. The use of this program for only this reason is both a mismanagement of funds, and a poor strategy for two reasons: (1) There is no way that the legislature will pay more money to have private citizens go in a perform these tasks, and (2) many of these jobs could be with a little more investment, ones that yielded certificates of training which would qualify these inmates for jobs of a similar nature on the outside.

Fairness and Humaneness

It was clear that this prison attempted to be humane, with one inmate per cell, and less crowded conditions in general. One might even be led to argue that the mere presence of a new prison is a testament to the state's willingness to be humane.

As for fairness, we were assured by our guide that in comparison to the days when he first started to work for the States Corrections Department that they were ultimately more fair than in the past. He told us of the procedure of individual guards locking inmates in their cells for days with no need of any approval. We were also alerted to the fact that now there is a grievance procedure where inmates may appeal practices by the staff, that there is an attorney at the facility, and that now inmate employment takes into consideration the percent of Blacks at the different job levels trying to strike some parity. The above all seem like the corrections department has made ultimate strides in this area.

On the other hand, how fair and humane can a prison be given our experiences with this person? The first problem is that we were just told how the program worked, we were not able to observe them. A second problem which calls humanness and fairness into question, is that we were not allowed an opportunity to speak with any inmates. The third and final problem is that after glancing at the brochure we were given about what inmates' families could bring them; how fair and humane can an institution be that makes rules for the sake of making rules?

Policy Changes

After reviewing pages of policy changes, we considered a question: what are some viable policy changes which the prison might implement for improvement? The first and largest policy change needed is for prisons individually, and departments of corrections collectively are to open themselves up to objective, professional evaluation and study. This point is essential, because if prisons are really interested in more than serving as a Skinnerian laboratory, then it is very important to get new and fresh ideas brewing. In other words, it is inordinately difficult for constructive criticism, and change in a vacuum.

A second area which needs especially to be changed at this prinson is the waste of opportunity to actually train people in an "on the job training type of way." Here the point is, true they use inmates as clerks, plumbers, carpenters, and maintenance men in general, but with no certification what chances do these inmates have of obtaining meaningful employment.

The final area is in the area of restrictions. It is true that if one is to have institutions which are to house and control large numbers of people it is necessary to have rules. But one must also keep in mind that rules on top of rules for no reason can reach a point of diminishing returns. For instance, is there any reason which you can see that a prison administrator should be worried about how many pairs of underwear an inmate can receive from their families, or when is the next time they can get another pair from their families? It is my guess, in this case, that prison administrators can surely find something better to do with their time.

ACHIEVEMENT HOUSE
A RESEARCH NARRATIVE

PROJECT GOALS

1. To develop a family type community residence for young men in danger of placement in a secure facility.
2. To assist home residents, males ages 13-17 in acquiring social and school skills needed to ensure well function in community life.
3. To end further adjudication of program residents by the juvenile justice system.
4. To offer natural parents the opportunity to acquire the skills needed to maintain and nurture clients upon their return home.

POPULATION TO BE SERVED
AND HOW THEY WILL BE OBTAINED

The population we are to serve will consist of adjudicated youths, ages 13-17 (race, religion and ethnic backgrounds do not matter). Our rationale for excluding females was that males project more fear and there are more available statistics on male behaviors, treatments, etc., to help us plan, implement and evaluate our program. However, we do not intend to be sexist—once the male Achievement House was under way, we would turn our attention to females and focus solely on them.

Male youths are selected at random for the program from a pool of eligible adjudicated males. The criteria used to select these boys includes: age (13-17 years old); reside within the county of the Achievement will already occurred. Program youth must have failed to positively respond to probation or counseling services available to him and the youth must have a family in the community to return to. This would exclude youths who have committed certain violent offenses (murder, forcible rape and armed robbery) because of community sentiments against these serious offenders; are addicted to dangerous narcotics (heroin, barbiturates, etc.) and require medical care, which Achievement Place wouldn't be staffed to supervise, as well as anyone with a serious physical disability, which would also require other types of care or extensive training in a related health field.

TYPE OF PROGRAM

The type of program Achievement Place would host is a community based, residential, family-style (teaching-parents and male youth), group home treatment program (these youths require more supervision than probation) for eight adjudicated males, ages 13-17. The average length of stay at Achievement Place would range from nine to twelve months, and would depend on the youth's progress. (If a youth was ready to leave before that time period, we would certainly assist him in his move—this is because it isn't wise to keep a youth at Achievement House when he is ready to move on.)

Our program would also utilize alternative schools because anyone can attend these schools (they do not have to reside in the particular school district). The reason this is pointed out is because the length of stay at Achievement House can vary among the male youths. For example, if a male leaves Achievement House in February, and returns to his family's house while school is in session, he can still attend the same school because it doesn't matter where the family lives.. Therefore, there wouldn't need to be a disruption in the youth's life caused by his changing

89

schools. Also, a lot of these youths lack certain basic academic skills—alternative schools provide remedial classes to help correct this.

The project will be administered by a Task Force which will report to the Board of Directors of the state. This Task Force, with the addition of other community volunteers will eventually form the independent governing board of this project.

LENGTH AND PHASING OF THE PROGRAM

One point which should remain in everyone's mind, when talking of length and phasing of a program, is that nothing is set in concrete until the plan is further developed. This is to say that often a plan may be tentative. The main ideological point of organization can be found in that different individuals are able to progress at different rates than others. For this reason, both the rate in which our program is phased, and the length of time it takes an individual to progress through our program will be set at an individual indeterminate pace.

From the above ideological position, it should not be gathered that the program is totally subjective. Guidelines on how long it takes an individual to get through the program. The average amount of time it should take someone to journey through the program is from 9-10 months, but take note that this is not a rule (if an individual progresses at a faster rate than they will be released faster).

The reason for this indeterminate length of the program is for treatment rather than punishment. If one sets a determinate length of time in a sentence then there is little incentive for real attitude change, for no reward is given if this change occurs. On the other hand, if one utilizes indeterminate sentencing the participant's length of stay is dependent on the progress made so that there is plenty of incentive for improvement.

The indeterminate length of the program with guidelines of 9-10 months of residence allow for the programs' phasing. The program starts with a strict behavior modification technique of a token economy, with hopes of moving towards the end of the program, to a more self-directed motivation system. s the participants adjust their behavior toward more socially accepted forms, they are slowly pushed to a more self[-]directed frame of evaluation. This is done generally at first with evaluation and reward coming at short intervals, and as the participant progresses rewards are administered at longer and longer intervals.

The specifics of how the evaluation and reward intervals might work in this way is, at first the participant is evaluated and rewarded daily for privileges. Then as the participant progresses the evaluation and reward interval is prolonged until it is more along the lines of the merit system. It should be mentioned that at these latter stages the participant is working toward spending more time at home or in their foster home. This is not just serving as a reward it is also serving as a means to ease the participant into the environment that they will face after the program has ended. The participants will not be simply thrown into an environment in which they are to survive, but will be phased into this environment.

TECHNOLOGY

"The function of the Achievement House Program is to help youths who are in danger of institutionalization remain in their communities." (Stumphauzer, p. 120) Several types of technology utilized at Achievement Place combine with each other to achieve this goal. The treatment program is run by a couple, referred to as "teaching-parents" was invented to distinguish them from the traditional, custodial house-parents or foster parents who do not have the same training or skills as teaching-parents). These teaching-parents have two main roles. One is to "develop positive personal teaching relationships with their youths, enabling them to teach the behavior skills likely to produce positive community reaction" and the other is "to assume responsibility for the youths and become their advocates in the community. (Stumphauzer, p. 120) The teaching-parents try to provide a nurturing atmosphere in which it is possible to

Cynthia Price

teach and improve a youth's behavior and skills. The behavioral skills training program at Achievement House consists of four main elements: 1) a motivation or token economy system, 2) a self-governing system, 3) a comprehensive behavioral skills training curriculum, and 4) the development of a reciprocally reinforcing relationship between the youths and the teaching-parents. (Stumphauzer, p. 121)

The motivation or token economy system monitors the behavior of the youth and helps the youth to learn and establish more positive behaviors (in and out of school). This is accomplished by a point system, which every youth engages in from the moment he enters Achievement Houseto the day he leaves. To motivate a youth to adopt appropriate behaviors, he is given points for every positive behavior he exhibits. For example, a youth obtains points by successfully completing his homework, cleaning his room, and avoiding fights in school. He, in turn, loses points for engaging in any negative behaviors or regressing to old patterns, which have repeatedly caused him to get into trouble. For instance, a youth could lose points by acting out in the group home, by refusing to wash the dishes when it is his turn, by receiving a bad report card, by causing trouble in his classroom at school. The points a youth earns (computed on a daily basis first and on a weekly basis later, when the youth's behaviors have improved and he has earned the rights to graduate to weekly point system) can be exchanged for privileges such as night time snacks, an allowance of some sort, the freedom to spend weekends with the youth's natural or foster parents at their homes, (the more points obtained, the more freedom the youth can exercise and, therefore, motivation to adopt appropriate behaviors will naturally increase). Once the youth has shown success with the daily and weekly points system, he can then graduate to the merit system, in which there aren't any points to exchange for privileges—the privileges are still given by the teaching-parents but only on the premise that the youth maintains his positive behaviors (if positive remain stable, the youth will be able to spend more and more time with his family until he is finally released from Achievement Place). If the youth slips, however, he will return to the point system and privileges will be taken away.

The second element of technology is the self-government system, which means that the youths can and do participate in the direction and operation of the Achievement House Program—this is usually accomplished at the daily family conference meetings, which occur after dinner. Here the youths can democratically discuss what constitutes appropriate and inappropriate behaviors, who has exhibited what types of behaviors and the consequences of these behaviors, and a change to review the peer manager (this person is chosen through a democratic election by all the youth) who "oversees and teaches routine social and self-help skills." (Stumphauzer, p. 122) These meetings provide the opportunity for a youth to vent his feelings and frustrations concerning Achievement Place, the teaching-parents, his peers, and to openly confront and deal with these feelings in the correct and appropriate manner. While these meetings proceed, the teaching-parents teach the youths such skills as constructive criticism, problem solving, negotiation, and interpersonal skills.

Another technological element involves the comprehensive behavioral skill training curriculum. Here the teaching-parents teach the youth appropriate behavioral skills interpersonal, social, academic, prevocational, and self-care skills through positive and negative reinforcement, modeling, and instruction so that they can eventually return to their homes instead of being sent to detention homes or elsewhere—these new, positive behavioral skills will help the youth to adapt to the world and people around him in a constructive manner. The daily report card that a youth takes to school and has his teacher fill out at the end of the school day (simple yes and no evaluative questions are asked) are brought home and are reviewed by the teaching-parents, who use these report cards to monitor the youth's behavior while he is away at school (if the point system is being utilized with this youth, he can either receive points or lose them depending on whether his report card was good or bad, respectively). The teaching-parents help each individual youth in their particular behavioral problem area(s) at night or whenever possible (there are usually counseling sessions at night designed to accomplish this goal). Throughout the entire day, the youth receives constant feedback about

Cynthia Price

his behavior and is reinforced accordingly (a lot of encouragement is given to the youths, especially concerning their interpersonal social skills, since there is an area in which most of the youth require more help).

The fourth element, the development of a reciprocally reinforcing relationship between the youth and the teaching-parents, provides the framework for the whole program. When this type of mutual relationship exists it helps both parties to get along with each other and work toward the same goal. It provided a nurturing atmosphere and stable environment in which the youths and teaching-parents can be friends and respect one another (the youths are more willing to adopt positive behaviors within this type of environment.).

During the school year we wouldn't want any of our youths to hold jobs because most have deficient academic skills and need to concentrate on their studies to improve these skills. However, we would urge the boys to get jobs in the summer so that they could keep busy, gain responsibility, and earn some money for themselves (especially the older boys, due to the fact that they will be entering the job market sooner and will need as many skills as they can possibly attain). We would ask community agencies to help place these boys into available jobs if funding was available.

Older males might not have any idea of what they want to do in the way of a career—even if they do have an idea, they might feel that it's impossible to attain their dream (due to lack of role models, education, finances). The program proposes to have career models (i.e., black doctors, Hispanic engineers, white lawyers) come to Achievement House and talk about their particular fields, what it is like to be a majority/minority in that field, what the youths will need to acquire these jobs (i.e., education, financial resources, types of experience), so that the youths can start to think about their futures and formulate some realistic goals. The program will also try to provide some career models who were once youth offenders themselves so that our youths could identify with these men and realize that they, too, can make it out in the real world.

94

Along with career modeling, we feel it is important to establish some type of job club in order to teach our male youth basic job skills to prepare them for the job market. These job skills would include the following: writing resumes, what to say and what not to sat at interviews, (the teaching-parents could develop several role playing sessions for the youths to examine different interviewing settings and how to respond to them), how to dress for interviews, how to write letters to sell one's skills and self to companies or agencies that interest them, etc. We would also work on self-confidence, assertiveness, and other similar skills. With these basic skills behind them, our youths will feel more confident about going out into the job market, and will hopefully be in a better position to secure a job.

STAFFING AND STAFF DEVELOPMENT

Achievement House should have five staff members. The first staff member would be the Project Coordinator who must possess a M.S.W. or a D.S.W. Our rationale for selecting a candidate with one of these degrees is that we want a highly qualified person with a human services, educational background, whose social skills are professionally geared toward clients as well as administrators (M.S.W. or D.S.W. workers have usually had more experience and training in their fields and would, therefore, be in a much better position to handle this type of responsibility). The project director's responsibilities will include: conducting outreach, providing linkages with the outside community, networking, educating the community about Achievement Place (i.e., public meetings), taking care of fiscal functions (i.e., auditing) and administrative tasks, conducting parent training groups (i.e., help the parents of the Achievement Place youth to adjust to their child coming home), and providing on-going training for the teaching-parents. We will provide one F.T.E. (full-time equivalent) for the project director.

Achievement House will also hire two teaching-parents (two F.T.E.s) who must possess a B.A. in Social Work, Psychology or Sociology. The rationale for hiring someone with one of these degrees would be similar to the project directors—the difference being that the teaching-parent position would not require as much experience or training (remember that the project director would be responsible for providing on-going training for the teaching-parents). The teaching-parents will provide a nurturing atmosphere for the male youths and teach social (especially interpersonal) skills as well as academic skills (assist the youths with their homework in ways which will help them to learn and retain academic information and skills). The teaching-parents will also act as role-models and counselors for the youths. They will reside at Achievement House and work around the clock except for when the childcare worker relieves them.

One F.T.E. will be provided for a childcare worker. Actually, we prefer to split the F.T.E. in half and hire two childcare workers part-time. These childcare workers (custodial Help) would be similar to foster parents (no degree will be required) and they would relieve the teaching-parents when the teaching-parents needed time off or needed to attend a conference, etc. The child care workers will be trained by the certificated children's agency.

Our last employee will be a part-time secretary (.25 F.T.E. will be allowed for this position) who will help the project director with paperwork and any other duties which are deemed necessary. If possible, a part-time counselor for Children at Risk and a records secretary should be hired to help with the project. The House also needs maintenance aids (to help with plumbing, ground work, electrical problems, etc.).

To provide additional training for the teaching-parents, we will have social workers come in periodically and lecture on issues such as racism, sexism, etc. We will also bring in an education advocate who will teach the teaching-parents and project coordinator how to work with and use the public schools (since Achievement House staff will have close contact with the public schools on behalf of their youth). Finally, we will provide legal training for Achievement House staff so that they will be equipped to deal with any legal matters as they occur (youths getting into trouble at schools, creating a minor offense).

FUNDING

Federal funding sources Government funds for all or parts of this program can be sought through the Department of Social Services, or ought directly from the Federal Department of Health and Human Services. Funds can also be sought from private foundations.

Funds under this title could be sought for development of new strategies for <u>Group Homes for Dependent Children</u> and basic research on <u>Children in Institutions</u>. Funds for this title are part of the Adoption Assistance and Child Welfare Act of 1980. They can be used "on behalf of eligible children who need care away from families (in foster care) who are in the placement and care of the state agency administering the program and to provide Federal Financial participation in the cost of proper and efficient administration and training costs.

There could be mental health funds available for this program (upon research). The current position is that each department will offer treatment to delinquent and/or adjudicated adolescents if they are in extreme danger of inflicting harm to themselves or are exhibiting other psychotic symptoms of magnitude that clear no other setting but mental health institutionalization is suitable.

Finally, in order to provide parenting for the skills training component for parents of clients, funds will be sought from private foundations. Rationale for application will be that these funds will provide for the education and retraining which will allow and or enhance the ability of natural parents to receive their youth back home and to continue successfully to keep them at home.

Cynthia Price

GOVERNANCE OF THE PROGRAM

The particular issue of governance of this program, the particular question of how this might be structured in a fashion which will provide a valuable educational lesson to the participants in our program. With this in mind, it occurs to the authors of this program that this would entail optimal participation by the participants it is evident that with the above question it seems the only way to proceed is some form of participant self-government.

At this point it is wise to explain what makes this decision so evident from an educational point of view. The first point which should be made along these lines is that this does not have to necessarily mean chaos. This is mainly for the reason that reasonably fair rules can be assumed to be forged simply because each participant must live in this environment for some time, and little advantage can be achieved by the constituting of a ridiculous system of rules. Also with a system where all have a say in the valuation of all, it is certain to develop both a skill of both giving constructive criticism, and benefiting from criticism. It is clearly important to emphasize that this is a skill which is essential for the adjusting of behavior to more socially accepted forms.

As for the mechanics as to how this participant self-governing system will be run, the authors have conceived of it in the following manner: (1) a daily meeting which would review appropriate and non[-]appropriate behavior, and comment specifically on these types of behaviors among individuals in the program, and (2) daily election of a peer manager whose behavior exemplifies the behavior which is to be reinforced through the program to supervise and teach social and self[-]help skills to other participants. Here it is seen with these two mechanisms working that you both foster an acceptance of evaluation, and you hinge success on fulfillment of socially acceptable forms of behavior (which are two of our foremost goals).

RACISM AND SEXISM

The problem of racism and sexism are very real problems, and not problems to be cast aside while the things which seem of immediate importance are dealt with. It seems in this regard that the best way to avoid these problems is to plan specific policies from the initial planning of the program into when the particular program is well established. With this in mind it is the persuasion of our program to operate in this way in the planning of how to avoid racism and sexism in our program.

Some of the first decisions along these lines to consider are the composition of the board and who is hired as teaching parents. Here it is important to emphasize the importance that these groups be balanced along the lines of race and sex. This is especially important because these are persons who will implement the founding policies of the program, and if there is only one type of person on these bodies, do not be surprised if racism and sexism emerges. This does not mean that the policies suggested will have these ends in mind, but they just will not be as sensitive to needs which emerge because of race and sex.

As for policies or practices which should be enacted in the context of a more everyday framework we have these suggestions: (1) Black, White, female, role models, (2) school system which the composition of its' staff has these concerns in mind, (3) the food served, (4) activates of the program, and (5) the music and pictures displayed in the house. In the case of the first suggestion it is very important that when one invites role models to speak in the house that some sort of balance along these lines is kept. With the second suggestion it helps a great deal to have a school system which has equitable rations of blacks, whites, males and females as teachers. As for the food which is served a certain amount of variety in types of food will go a long way in heading off racial tension, this is to say one night is soul food night, one night is Mexican food night, etc. Along the lines of the fourth suggestion, what is meant here is that there should be a certain awareness of ethnic activities, practices, and holidays. And the final consideration is that there be a variety of differing types of music available, and that respect is given to heroes of all genders, races, and creeds. With what was just mentioned it is hoped through exposure that this will make the participant sensitive and aware of other customs and practices which they otherwise might not have an opportunity to be made aware of.

PLAN FOR COPING WITH POLITICAL OPPOSITION

When we think of the topic of political opposition we first think of what areas of the city we can realistically enter with the least resistance regarding renting, zoning laws, and last of all: how to calm future neighbors. Although this prioritizing of barriers to be overcome is not meant to mean that community relations are unimportant, but that zoning and obtaining a lease are more pressing issues requiring attention immediately. Also along these lines it is believed that neighbors' opinions will be most affected by what they see after the program has moved in. This strategy is advocated mainly because it is not possible to locate a program for juvenile offenders in a multitude of places, and preliminary community opinion on programs of this nature are always negative in the beginning.

The first phase of this project is that of obtaining a house in an appropriately zoned district. At this point of the process it may be necessary to have a larger damage deposit than an average tenant, because landlords may have apprehension attached to leasing their property to a program of this type. But most important is to make sure one is renting in an area which is zoned for dwelling units for groups of unrelated persons. The areas zoned for such purposes are residential zones with the number four in the code, office zones, local business zones, campus service zones, commercial residential zones, and fringe commercial zones.

For the purposes of this project we have chosen to locate in a residential zone with the number four contained in the code. These areas are called Multiple Family Dwelling Units. The reason this classification of the zone code was chosen was guided by the factors of least resistance to our program, and that of cost. With this in mind it is very doubtful that within the local business, campus business, office, or fringe commercial districts that we would: (1) find a landlord willing to lead to our program, or (2) find a living unit within our price range.

The advantage of locating in the residential zones which we intend, is that these are areas with large numbers of students populating them. This is an advantage for two reasons: (1) students tend to be short term residents of particular living units, and are not likely to put up as much community opposition as more permanent residents, (2) that from a largely student population it may be possible to tap their expertise.

As for the exact location of this house for the program, as close as we can come at this point are general areas of Ann Arbor. At this point given our educational goal to work with high community high schools it would be an advantage to be as close to this facility as possible. With the proximity of a community high school very important on our list of priorities we propose to locate between the boundaries for the proposed area.

The next problem is one of diffusing community opposition. This is no easy task, realistically with some we will just have to say we're here, and no matter how much you dislike us we will continue to stay here. But in large the majority we can win over by such functions as open houses, and trying to get volunteers from the community. Here it is our plan to first hold an open house, this is so that the community may have an opportunity to see what the purpose of the house is. After this initial stage an aggressive campaign to enlist volunteers must be launched for volunteers to show community support. During this volunteer program it is also necessary to educate the public through brochures about the performance of other programs of our nature, and through public speaking engagements. Through these efforts to both involve, and inform the community it is our prediction that we will become acceptable.

Cynthia Price

PUBLICITY AND PROJECT INTERPRETATION

Most advocates of community based residential programs are fortunate that many desirable residential areas within the city are zones to allow unrelated groups of persons to live together in a single dwelling. Because of this, political campaigns to achieve favorable zoning can be eliminated. If the program is able to find and rent a suitable building for the program residence, there should be no legal barriers to occupancy following needed renovations to bring the property up to health and safety codes.

However, despite plans to acquire a residence, much of the success of this program will depend on its integration with the larger community. At first, in order to gain neighborhood acceptance of our future residents, a door to door outreach campaign will take place within a three square block range on all sides of the residence home. This outreach will be planned to acquaint neighbors with goals of the program and with the activities of the program. The planned outcome of this activity will be that fears in the neighborhood will be reduced and that, albeit possibly not universal, support for project goals will be gained. In order to reduce neighbor fears, neighbors will be given the name of a staff person to contact in future should questions and/or concerns arise. Staff all be able to furnish data about programs in other communities.

In order to network with and to gain support, the program directors will allocate his/her time in support of the activities in the community and whenever time allows will allocate time for contribution to the work of others appropriate child welfare activities in said area. The program director will act as liaison to the County Juvenile Court, both closely monitoring the client selection process and in obtaining feedback about program functioning and outcomes from the court. The program coordinator will work with county police persons in order to gain both their understanding of program goals and to gain their understanding of ways program youth will be relating to the community. Police will be asked to follow certain procedures with program clients should they become involved with them in either an official or unofficial capacity.

A single staff person will be the liaison with Public Schools administrators although it is expected that program counselors will relate to specific teachers when necessary to support the school experience of a resident.

Staff will actively seek opportunities to explain the goals and activities of the program to church members, social and fraternal groups, civic groups and city and county government officials. Further, staff will access the printed and electronic media including public access TV in order to continuously interpret the program to the community. The outcome of these efforts will be citizen support and understanding of the program and the obtaining of volunteer support by area citizens as well as financial contributions for use for such items and recreation and equipment not provided by program funders.

In order to comply with the Freedom of Information Act and in order to further promote understanding of the outcomes of the use of the Achievement House Model, data will be furnished to interested researchers in addition to data provided to program funders. Staff will cooperate with researchers who comply with institutional human subject research guidelines in all ways possible within the constraints of client confidentiality.

PLANS FOR STABILIZATION OVER TIME

The success of this project is predicated upon a program life spanning several funding years. Admissions and discharges will be based on client need rather than restrictions imposed by the parameters of a fiscal year. Implicit in initial negotiations with any funder will be long range sustenance of the project and all attempts will be made to obtain initial three year funding commitments from the federal government and/or state angencies.

Long range success of the project also rests upon its ability to integrate with the community in order to assure any needed support for former program clients and their families. Thus, relationships will be established with the courts, schools, recreation, family counseling services and programs offering youth employment. The agency director will work with any local planning agencies such as United Way and Community Action Agency toward support for funds and toward integration of project services into the community human services infrastructure.

It is planned that our parent education groups will be available to individuals referred from other community agencies, thus increasing the ties of the project to the larger service community. Program personnel will remain, when necessary, available to school people to act in support of program clients following their return home.

Volunteers will be enlisted to serve on the Board of Directors and as program support staff. Training to facilitate volunteer skill growth and commitment to the project will be ongoing. It is planned that volunteers, both, lay and professional, will act as community advocates for the continuation of the project. Outside evaluation will be employed to further support funders expected positive results of program activities.

Plans to secure continued support include ongoing access of printed and electronic media and continued relationships with state and county legislators and members of appropriate legislative committees such as Judiciary, Appropriations, Education and Health and Human Services.

EVALUATION

Evaluation of the effect of the program on clients is predicated on two major premises. The first is that there will be an unbiased, random selection of the boys who will enter the Achievement House Project. The second is that criteria for education achievement and social adjustment will be stated and the outcomes on these dimensions for Achievement House clients will be quantified by objective standards.

Young med selected to enter Achievement House will have been adjudicated to a secure program. Their alternative assignment to Achievement House will provide boys already in the correction system the least secure placement possible resulting from the adjudication. The selection of a youth to fill the vacancy will be based on selecting a candidate from the next three adjudicated youth who fill the program criteria. Following notification to the Juvenile Court of a vacancy in the program, any three youth men who meet program age criteria (12-17), who have not committed a crime beyond the magnitude permitted to program participants, and who are neither mentally retarded or substance addicted will be eligible. From this group of three young men, two will be randomly selected to be in the control group and will be sent to a program as mandated by the sate and one will be assigned to Achievement House Young men comprising a control group will be evaluated and the results of tests administered to them as well as their adjudication rates will be used as a base upon which to compare the results of the Achievement House program.

During their stay at Achievement House, young men will be administered standardized tests to evaluate their attitudes and achievements on several levels. These tests will be chosen in consultation with professors from the State of Education and Department of Psychology. Although the literature cites tests used previously, the fluid state of the art in evaluation mandates that this consultation be used in order that the evaluators use the most current and accurate evaluation tools. Control group youth in secure facilities will be administered like these unless they are no longer available to program testers. (END of Sentence and change of state residence will be considered possible and adequate reasons for not administering a test to a control group member.) Tests will yield results on the following:

- Achievement orientation of youth
- Internal control level responsiveness to external controls
- Sense of self-worth
- Communication skills.

In addition to standardized tests, school grades of Achievement House youth will be compared to grades of peers in school. It is planned that Achievement House youth will perform at least median level in all classes in which they are enrolled.

Finally, for two years following the original adjudication, adjudication records for both the experimental and control group will be maintained in said state. Achievement House youth will be adjudicated at a rate 75% lower than the control group youth.

Parent groups will be evaluated according to assessment of parent satisfaction with skills taught. Additionally, before and after tests will be developed to be administered to ascertain growth in such parenting skills as:

- Behavior confrontation and change.
- Communication skills.
- Knowledge of normal teenage development.
- Appropriate parental assertion.

REFERENCES

About - Interaction Institute for Social Change : Interaction Institute for Social Change

Airasian, Peter W. "Educational Testing in Public Policy: Growth and Implications." Address delivered for "The Individual, the Environment, and Education: A Conference in Honor of Benjamin S. Bloom," University of Chicago, March 2-3, 1984.

Ann Arbor Department of City Planning Zoning and Reference Maps.

Bourdieu, P. (1986). "The forms of capital," pp. 241-58 in: J.G. Richardson (ed.): *Handbook for Theory and Research for the Sociology of Education.*

Bronfenbrenner (1994). Chapter 5: Ecological models of human development. In International Encyclopedia of Education. Volume 3, 2nd edition. Pages 37-43.

Brownmiller, Susan, Against Our Will, Bantam Books I.n.c., 1975.

Clemmer, Donald, (1958) The Psion Community, Holt, Rinehart and Winston.

Coleman, James (1988). Social capital in the creation of human capital. 80 - 96.

Cross, C. (2004). *Political /education National Policy Comes of Age.* New York, New York: Teacher College Press.

Eitzen, D. Stanley. "The Effects of Behavior Modification on the Attitudes of Delinquents" in Progress in Behavior Therapy With Delinquents, Jerome S. Stumphauzer, Editor. Charles C. Thomas, Illinois, 1979.

Fixsen, Dean L.; Phillips, Elery L. and Montrose, M. Wolf. "Achievement Place: Experiments in Self-Government with Pre-delinquents." Journal of Applied Behavior Analysis. Spring 1973.

Guralnik, David B. Webster's New World Dictionary, William Collins and World Publishing Co., Inc., 1973.

Gurin, Patricia, Epps, Edgar, Black Consciousness, Identity, and Achievement, John Wiley & Sons, Inc, 1975.

Gutmann, A. (1987). *Democratic Education*. Princeton, New Jersey: Princeton University Press.

Hill, Freddye, "The Nature and Context of Black Nationalism at Northwestern in 1971", Journal of Black Studies, 1975, 5, pp. 320-336.

http://education.ohio.gov/getattachment/Topics/Testing/Sections/Related-Information/Testing-Report-and-Recommendations-2015-1.pdf.aspx

http://education.ohio.gov/Topics/Testing/
English-Language-Arts-and-Mathematics)

http://www.theohstandard.org/standards101 Ohio Department of Education Ohio Standardized Testing 101

INTERVIEWS- Office of Children and Youth Services, Michigan Department of Social Services, November 1982, Washtenaw County Community Mental Health December,1982. Washtenaw County Community Mental Health December,1982. Clinical Director, Orchards Children's Services, Livonis, Michigan, November, 1982. Program Director, Boysville of Michigan, December, 1982.

Irwin, John, (1980) <u>Prisons in Turmoil</u>, Little Brown Company. Jacobs, James, <u>Stateville</u>. (1977). The University of Chicago Press. Jacobs, James, (1974) "Street Gangs Behind Bars", <u>Social Problem</u>, 21. pp. 305-409

Koffler, Stephen L. "Statewide Testing Programs: From Monitors of Change to Tools of Reform." Paper presented at the annual meeting of the National Council of Measurement in Education, New Orleans, April 1984.

Leonard (2011). Using Bronfenbrenner's ecological theory to understand community partnerships: A historical case study of one urban high school. Urban Education. Volume 46, Issue 5. Pages 987 – 1010.

Leonard, J. (2011). Using Bronfenbrenner's ecological theory to understand community partnerships: A historical case study of one urban high school. Urban Education, 0042085911400337.

Michigan Department of Correction, (1980) <u>Annual Statistical Report</u>.

O'Donnell, P. (2015, July 1). Ohio picks AIR to replace just-ousted for Common Core tests. *The Plain Dealer*.

Pitts, James P., "Politicalization of Black Students: Northwestern University" <u>Journal of Black Studies</u>, Mar.,1975. pp. 277-319

Pitts, James P., "The Politicalization of Black Students", <u>Journal of Black Studies</u>, 1975, 5, pp. 277-319.

Pitts, James P., "The Study of Race Consciousness: Comments on New Direction", <u>American Journal of Sociology</u>, 1974, 80, pp. 665-687.

Price, C. (2019). <u>150 50: a teacher's account of urban schools</u> - DORRANCE PUB CO.

<u>prince ea youtube - Search (bing.com)</u>

Quotations from interviews conducted by Richard J. Tabler from 1/83-2/83

Rosenthal, S.J. "Symbolic Racism and Desegregation". Phylon, Sept. 1980. pp. 257-266

"Racial and Ethnic Achievement Gaps", Stanford Center for Education Policy Analysis, Center for Education Policy Analysis Stanford University 2015

Research in Rural Education, Volume 3, Number 1, 1985 Rural and Urban Teachers: Differences in Attitudes and Self Concepts LANDA L. TRENTHAM I AND BARBARA B. SCHAER

Rivlin, Alice M. "Forensic Social Science." Harvard Educational Review 43, no. 1 (1973): 61-75.

Sykes, Gresham, (1958) The Society of Captives. Princeton University Press.

Stone, D. (2012). *Policy Paradox The Art of Political Decision Making* (Third ed.). New York: W. W. Norton & Company.

Tabler, Richard J., Fleming, Garry, Allen, Walter R., "Predominantly White Universities and their Effect on Group Consciousness", presented at the annual meeting of The American Educational Research Association, Montreal, Canada, 1983, pp. 1-21.

Trent, R. "Background/History of Ohio Proficiency Tests." Ohio Department of Education (1998, September 18). from http://www.chuh. net/school/FAQs/OPTs.background.html

Tyack, D. (2003). *Seeking Common Ground Public Schools in a Diverse Society.* Cambridge, Massachusetts: Harvard University Press.

Walker, T. (2015). Poll: Americans Want Less Standardized Testing and More School Funding. *News and Features from the National Education Association NeaToday.*

Milton Keynes UK
Ingram Content Group UK Ltd.
UKHW020941120424
440994UK00013B/297

9 798823 020886